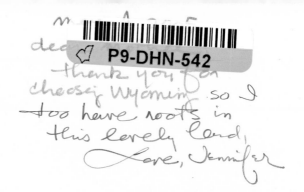

P9-DHN-542

thank you for choosing Wyoming so I too have roots in this lovely land, Love, Jennifer

Ancestors in the Landscape

By Maureen Tolman Flannery

John Gordon Burke Publisher, Inc.

Dedicated to
my father Dean Tolman
who blessed me
with a childhood in this landscape
and
to my cousin Dan Tolman
who shared with my children
his ranch knowledge
and the chance to trail sheep.

Library of Congress Cataloging-in-Publication Data

Flannery, Maureen Tolman, 1947-
  Ancestors in the landscape / by Maureen Tolman Flannery.
     p. cm.
  ISBN 0-934272-80-8 (alk. paper)
  1. West (U.S.)--Poetry. 2. Ranch life--Poetry. 3. Family--Poetry. I. Title.

  PS3556.L365A53 2004
  811'.54--dc22   2004007977

Credits: Cover Design by Gia Davis.

Copyright©2004 by Maureen Tolman Flannery
All Rights Reserved
Printed and bound in the United States of America

Contents

WESTERN LAND

Western Land

is not a commodity
isn't passive
isn't merely ridden over
fenced, proved up on
hayed, irrigated, grazed.
It coils around your sense of self
and rises up in gullies
like a striking diamond-back;
inserts mountainous power
into the inner workings of families
demanding that generations
which have dispersed like scattered herds
recline again on the same rocky bedground.
Subliminal as air
it becomes what you are thinking
without thinking about it.

Badlands

A brutal beauty informs these desert badlands
as if we substitute for an aesthetic
respect for the tenacity of all that cling to life
in such a barren stretch of earth—
scrubby sagebrush scenting arid air,
sparse tufts of vegetation loosely resembling grass
but graying to the color of the soil,
now checked as grandma's china in the kiln that is July,
prickly-pear cactus thriving on dryness
flaunting succulent yellow blossoms
as if daring us to pick,
a horned toad, barbed as his cactus shelter
and color-coded to the ground
as he scurries out of sight
in his hurry to go nowhere,
ants that have, in constructing their mound,
destroyed all growth in a wide girth,
leaving the already-unproductive earth
now, in rings, sterile as a gelding,
and one lone meadowlark whose song,
like some fan-tailed mating dance,
seems much too hopeful
for its setting or its circumstance.

Ways of Being Incorporated

A scrub juniper on Mahogany Butte
has been turned to a thorn bush
by a couple wraps of barbed wire
from a long-gone fence
whose barbs protrude from bark
just enough to gouge a hide.

There's a ponderosa pine on the Tolman ranch
where some tired pioneer
hung the broken haim of a harness on a branch.
The tree grew into it
till now the ball of rusted iron
points to the east like a swollen thumb.
Another trunk has lipped over
a used horseshoe like a snake's mouth
with a frog leg hanging out.

Behind the house the old wire clothesline
is completely eaten by the two
opposing cottonwood trees it wrapped around.
Now it emerges from the core of one
and shoots like a true arrow
into the other across the yard.

These trees, mouthed to the mountain
grow around and devour
hard things we try to constrain them with,
even our lives.

Left Behind

On a low ridge of plain between Reliance
and an infinite play of white and blue-gray clouds
an abandoned house stores phantoms
of an early settler's ranch intentions
within its battered box of exposed gray boards,
themselves a triumph of endurance,
impaled on a shaft of relentless sky
through the negative space of opposite window frames.
In every direction rolling hills of green
mound and slope down over the edge of the world
and beyond.

Wyoming

where every town
has a sign
at its entrance
  posting
    population
      and
    the elevation,
which exceeds it,
where there's room
for a cowboy
on every license plate
and in every bed
and each one
    drives a pickup
    wears a Stetson
    spits snoose
    uses a gun
on animals he cares for
when its time
and kills
when its time
with neither guilt
nor show of sentiment.

After a Hard Winter

Spring is being coaxed out of the land
like a reticent child required to kiss
the coffin of his dead grandmother.
Ditch fires feed air hungry for
the musty smell of old grass burning.
Colts and lambs leap their lack of
the weariness that clings like muddy manure
to boots of those who have weathered
the winter. Soiled remains of majestic drifts
ice themselves tenaciously to the shade of culverts.
The first farmers are in the fields with chisel plows
while their wives walk out-buildings
and groves of trees to assess
what bitter winter tried to take with her
as she went, wailing like a banshee,
to her long–awaited death.

Sun Dances with Color

We switchback through anonymous glimmers of night
and approach the pass as color
condensing out of black
concentrates in a rising red sphere, then disperses,
differentiates into timber, high meadow, wildflowers,
and sky that domes rose-gold over us.

Having snaked our mountain way down into Buffalo
we roll out onto the endless expanse of Wyoming
where blue sky competes with sage
for the term eternal.
The hills, dry and absorbent as corn starch,
despair of knowing water. Willie sings us past
the Tower that raises its stallion power behind bluffs.

All at once, as if rust buttes and deep green pines
were not enough, in a soft, unanticipated drizzle
there appears a shaft of vibrant color,
God's old promise of moderation, so radiant
in the sun it throws a spectrum shadow
out of the sky and down onto the hillside
in phantom hues, then grows to a perfect arch
so close with its colors that we,
if we pulled off the road,
could retrieve a cauldron of gold from a nearby gully.
But we are hypnotized by Sundance
framed in illumined color
and are gifted enough with the gentle rain.

Powerful Medicine

for Tolman Peter Flannery

Beneath wide azure skies
on a high plateau above rim rocks
flat limestone, laid out in an ancient arrow,
has pointed the way
to the circular place of healing.

He sits, Indian style,
in the hub-stone of a medicine wheel
calling on the knowledge of ancestors
gone into the firm certainty of black soil.
And when he opens his mouth
to voice what rises up
from the four-quadrant abling of the place,
an eagle glides over the ridge behind him
soars silent as belonging
high above the rightness of his being here.

Medicine Wheel

Toward the highest peak in the range you rise
climbing and climbing. You snake around mountains
ascending another and another
until you stand at the summit atop the world
barely a full step down from the thunderbird's dome.
The wind, constantly sweeping it clean,
threatens to blow you down where you belong.
But you have climbed so you cling
like the leaning scrub cedar.
You stand outside the fence with its rows of barbed wire
to keep your dusty boots
off sacred stones of the Medicine Wheel.
The whole thorny sphere is tied
with scarves and rags and pieces of clothing
like *milagros* in a church
something of the questor offered to the place.
Left by the Crow who came for the Sun Dance
a Blackfoot, perhaps, who journeyed
to atone some private omission
an Arapaho on a vision quest, Shoshone here
to hear from the spirit of their chief?
You rip your shirt tail and tie it with the others.
You do not know what it means, but you want to.
You walk around it studying six stone cairns
like ancient unused campfire beds
expectantly facing the rising sun. Can you see
Red Eagle standing at the hub by the buffalo skull
his people chanting their praise
young girls dancing up and down the spokes?
They ask the success of the hunt.

You count the spokes,
twenty-eight roads from the hub,
the center, the beginning of all.
Twenty eight tribes of the Sheepeater nation?
Twenty eight poles of the Medicine Lodge?
You do not know, nor the Crow,
nor the men from the University.
Do you feel the hunger of Chief Joseph,
the void in his belly drawing wisdom like a twister pulls?
Do you hear the prayers of Washakie
pleading for the grace to lead his wayfarer people
to the place of their confinement?
The wisdom of this mountain is silent as its stones
and ceaseless as the wind.
You look out over the valley.
Hundreds of miles lie peacefully
around you like sheep on a bedground--
foothills, badlands, valleys, rivers
more mountains so far they are phantoms.
But you are at the summit of the world
and all of creation rays out from here
like spokes from a wheel.

Linen

Wyoming sky
  like a sun-bleached cotton sheet
  is all you want over you
    on a summer night.

Big Horn Mountains

Every time I see them—looming
wise white-haired old men against the sky
ancestors of my bones
I wonder what love
could have been strong enough
to lure me away
what other primal instinct more intense
than this, the homing urge
that always draws me back to see them,
changeless and serene,
these bearded wise and silent fathers
of my mountain soul.

Western Sky

The domain of raptors
captor of rancher's reverie
plain of softly crenulated clouds
of held-in rain and drain-shaped tornados
able, in a breath, to take things back to heaven
like the angel of death.

COUNTING IN SHEEPMEN'S DREAMS

Family Ranch

This is old growth,
one organism like the aspen grove
sending new shoots to incite
companioning of ground and sky.

A child stands on ancestral lands
and life rises through rust-colored mud
into the soles of his feet
quartzes around his marrow-bone
throbs a rhythmic linking
in the gristle of the organs
by which he survives.

Ranch

Stone faced, mute, did you choose us
for the names of horses yet unsired
by the Arabian stud whose tail would arch
into blue sky above your buttes,

for the daisy chains little girls unborn
would weave in your upper meadows,
for addictions that would come into our blood
and be overcome between blizzard and thaw

and the lesser cataclysms of rock and clay?
Admonishing us to consider what matters, what lasts
your sage surface, mottled as paint ponies,
gives over degrees of your easy intimacy with sky.

Was it your intent to move us through you to it?
Transparent as mica, this layered geology lays open
its veins like a dressed-out buck—red clay
cliffs and canyons, gulch, creek and springs

timber, parks and outcroppings ancient as thought.
Inscrutable as God, you give up some secrets and
grass over others with the amnesia of sod.
Fenced out of expanse into identity, into our family

in the proving up, irrigated with their sweat,
you became companion in the lives of ancestors
who grew used and weathered working you.
You have entered the bones of those who grazed

and rested their livestock on your feed and stoney bedgrounds.
Still you remain inert as a rodeo arena while we
play out the go-rounds, spurring and holding
one-handed to the rope, landing in dry dust,

barely hurt, with our goose-egg, applause
and a mouth full of Ten Sleep dirt.

Mentors

All the hermits and holy men
of my formative youth
were alcoholic sheepherders
in self-imposed exile
left alone from year to year
from binge to binge
with none but goddesses
of timber and sagebrush,
with a horse, a dog
and their unacknowledged longings,
their only visitors the camp tender
come to move the sheep wagon
to new grazing ground and bring more grub
and we, the rancher's little girls
eager for adventure stories and the gift
of an empty Bull Durham bag—
unbleached muslin with a yellow drawstring
just right for holding a little doll
or an abrasive, thorned pet horned toad,
that prehistoric pilgrim from another age
that could cling three-fingeredly to cloth.

A herder perfected something of the weaver's art—
working the limitless yarn of thin, immaculate air
spun in the nearly-touchable sun
daily back and forth, in and out of the warp,
the confining sheep wagon
drab as slag, gray as February hay.
He chewed on this rhythm of contrast—
cloud-sheep in blue skies
his herd on green feed,

wood-stove grease on compartments
where his canned goods were stored;
daybreak eagle-racing his skittish horse,
warding off demon cravings
of the moon-dark night;
climbing the heights
crawling into his bedroll;
the mountain to conquer
the cave to transform.
He was the shuttle
and he wove his scratchy wool life.

These men held knowledge
not inferior to any priest's—
where the purest waters
spring icy from the depths of earth,
the kindness of the star-flung night,
how to jacket a motherless lamb
with the hide of another,
healing arts for scours
or a maggoty sore from a shearer's knick,
how to check yourself for ticks,
when to let sheep graze or bunch them
and where to send the dog if some aren't there,
ways of splitting logs, mounting bareback,
calling mountain gods to account,
beating the obvious odds at solitaire.

They showed us how to whittle pine,
turn quartz and limestone boulders
into monuments whose strange configuration
told rare passers-by
how we had spent long idle afternoons.

Beyond these things
they taught by paradox
for what I sensed in them
even as a child
who had not learned distinctions
was that they'd lived events so disparate
from the gentleness of sheep,
their sometimes ravings having evened out
the clean reliability of mountain sunrise.
They volleyed all their lives for balance
between responsible sobriety
and each year's two-week drunk
when they'd spend every dime
pawn saddle and rifle
befriend all manner of gold-digging women
perhaps sign my dad's name
to a few bad checks across the state
before returning humbly to our door
to dry out and go back to the mountains.

And there in the mountains year after year
they were my teachers and my friends,
each with his sheep wagon
in its predictable summer meadow—
matted as an artist's print in blue and purple
by lupine and shooting star,
each telling tobacco-stained stories,
each spitting snuff or rolling his own
and saving the tobacco bags
for my sister and me.

Shot with Expectation

I talked to Daddy on the phone.
He said Glen Kistner died.
They found him in his place
across the tracks
stiff-asleep on the floor beside the stove—
unrealized potential heavy in the air as mildew.
Frost on the dirty windows had
crept inside and crystallized his blood.
Unfed cats paced like panthers.

Daddy gave a reading
at the quiet graveside service.
I picture his warm words drifting upward,
clouds of tribute in the January air
like incense rising.

Glen herded sheep for us when I was a girl.
He came with a history that allured.
He spoke of West Point, far-off cities,
two world wars. Sure, herders always
had a story tucked in a tobacco pouch
but Glen's were nicotine as grasshopper spit
steamy as those dark, loud places
where Daddy'd go to fetch him
while I waited, wide-eyed, in the pickup.
Perhaps he was the first to conjure in me
stirrings that there were
such things as handsome men.
Once he told me he had had a wife.
She was a concert pianist.

I liked to imagine she might
come through town—on tour?
They'd meet in the Ram's Horn Cafe
and talk about past passion.

When I'd hung up the phone I took
a worn leather purse from my dresser drawer.
Inside, an Indian head penny—1902—
and a perfect obsidian arrowhead,
transparent as his windows,
sharp as the icicle fingers of the frost.
Like his, its beauty counted half its promise,
but like him also,
shot with expectation long ago,
it missed its mark.
It was a treasure even then when he found it
in the fullness of his upright stature.
He bent deep to pick it
from the rain-washed ground.

He didn't give it to me then.
Perhaps he doubted a child could appreciate
the rarity of such an artifact. But later,
when I'd grown, with the world outside Wyoming
wound around me like a python, I went home.
Daddy and I visited his cat-infested shack.
He made the proud, shy presentation—
that change purse with the only treasures
he had saved from any of his lives—
the penny and the arrowhead,
fragile as the wild flowers it had lain beside,
delicately worked to a point as sharp as pine.

No longer sharp for herding sheep,
he drank the lay off like the second whiskey shot
that goes down easier.
His work had warranted its own rough pride,
its sounds as crisp as quakin' asps
the air clear larkspur blue.
They'd kept his sheep camp stocked with food.
He could stay sober most of the year.
Now to descend from mountains to town
from home in all outdoors where arrowheads
reminded him how free the Indians had been
to musty-scented hovel too close to the bars.
In recent years, my father took him fishing
petted his flock of needy cats
dried him out on bottom days
remembered for him the handsome soldier
who'd come out west to take up herding sheep.

Daddy said the prayers beside his grave.
I asked him if the piano player came.

Mountain Oysters

Invasive, Skoal-stained teeth
drag out those pink-gray pearls of possibility
through the severed scrotum of the young
buck who is now a wether, who will never
ram next season's lambs
into the backside of passive ewes,
will never snort and hoove at their sides
while climbing towers of regeneration.

There in the bucket beside the corral
pile up those magic beans of maleness
trailing their subcutaneous tubing—
ducts that tunneled through the bodies' labyrinth
to meadows of unknown springs.

Cleaning them for dinner is a
time-consuming, meditative task.
Each sinewy tunic must be cut away.
What then pops out is
that inner mystery of potency,
the clear, smooth oval and,
pressed against the center
of what would be next,
a bulbous blue vein
attached like a swamp leech,
like a worm crawled up
from the other side of birth.

"Feed My Sheep"

*for Marvin Tolman, Wyoming sheep-rancher
killed in the crash of a private plane he had hired to fly him
over the Big Horn Mountains. He was looking for lost sheep
just a week before the opening of hunting season.*

I sense the badlands will be bare next spring
for only such seeds lying captive,
dormant in expectant earth since before
he walked their hills, will dare to sprout and flower.

Will fall winds on Onion Gulch
sweep aspen leaves that match his hair
into cushions at the base of pines,
blow circles round the cabin door
and whisper questions of his absence?
In October, when the hunters come
how many pronged and regal animals
will walk before a gun, still dazed by what they saw,
their instincts all distorted as the form
that fell into the timber in their midst
to swallow up the night in crackling red
and disappear in blackened stillness?

And what of those sheep he'd been searching for,
the lambs that just last spring he'd helped
escape the womb into yellow light on rusted buttes?
Like fairy-tale children, had they wandered
into the dark wood? How could they have known
their idleness would draw him there in such a way,
their needs propel him to that foreign state
of quiet helplessness?

Perhaps his sheep were first to find him.
Their ears were tuned to Canyon Creek on stones
and wind in pines. The loud, unnatural intrusion
led them quickly to the blaze that fed on him
who had to come, on him who'd kept them fed.

They must have huddled close for warmth
as frightened children, alarmed
to be caretakers of their own protector.
Were they then first to blanket him
with virgin wool, its lanolin-anointing
testimonial that he had roughly
answered that most gentle of requests
another dying Shepherd made
millennia before?

Sheepman Dead

for Marvin Tolman

I wonder if the old ewes
walked the bed ground aimlessly last night
bleating with purpose as if to call a lamb
lost hours down mountain on the trail.
Will they, unable to graze the browning autumn grass,
scatter, searching like his faithful sheepdog,
wondering and waiting?
To their next spring lambs, what memories
might they whisper that will swell to myth
the legend of him with autumn hair
who stormed his love through hot profanity
that blew the badlands free of tumbled weeds,
who shouted them to safety, lured predators after himself,
even engulfed demons to protect his sheep.

Will younger herders find them, one by one,
years later, with scours and sore mouth,
maggoty and bleating madly, their sparse matted wool
barely clinging to tired, brittle stick-bones,
crazed but searching still?
Will their carcasses mar fresh fragrant timber
with rank, decaying flesh to affront noses
of hunters he'll no longer join?

And then, when fleece in fluffs falls
odorless to the sides to mix with needles
and the rich black earth the prairie dogs mound up,
will their clean white ribs lie waiting, reaching up,
expecting his return,
motionless and silent in the sun,
and form a cradle there to rock him
when he comes?

Jacketing a Lamb

The ewe knows her lamb by its bleat
and by its scent,
not by the way its matted new wool clumps
onto oversized skin that hangs in wrinkles
along its back like an extra-large sweater
on a skinny child, or by its acrobatics
as it leaps fleetingly airborne above spring feed,
or by its wobbly Brome grass legs,
or the way its ears flag east and west
like needles of a compass;
no, only its sound and its smell,
her voice in its throat
and her milk in its body,
those she knows unmistakably,
can detect in a herd of thousands.
Lambs on the move can mother-up in minutes
with never a mistaken identity.

But if her lamb has died
and if some healthy lamb
has a mother with blue bag
or one who died in labor
or is just too perverse to nurse,
bent as she might be,
on disproving myths
about the easy-goingness of sheep,
the herder can skin her dead lamb,
the lamb with no more voice,

but only scent—
getting stronger by the minute—
and put that skin on the lamb
who still bleats for milk
for some hope of survival
but has a smell that no ewe recognizes.
He can put its forelegs through the holes
and dress it as with a second woolen overcoat
still bloody on the lining side
and rub some of the dead lamb's guts
on its head to enhance the smell.

The ewe at first noses around
this strangely costumed creature
nudges it with her head, is suspicious,
afraid to believe what she hopes.
But recognizing its smell, she relents,
rejoicing in the miracle of it and gives thanks
that her muttony old prayers were answered
that her failing lamb is standing again,
its voice somehow strangely altered
but its smell distinctly her own.
As the herder holds his breath
watching to see if his graft will take
she lets it suck.

The almost-bum-lamb, mothered again,
nurses noisily, foreknees bent,
its head wedged under to her bag.
Hind end in the air with its tail
waving and flopping like a flag on a stick
it roots like a rodent
burrowing, sucking her mothering
into its frail body.

By the time this ewe's milk has been digested,
the stinky decomposing jacket
can be thrown away.
Her watery white nurture
has navigated his intestines
and she's bound by her own identity
to let him stay.

The Trail

They have rounded up the ewes
and lambs born on the buttes
and bedded them in the beef pasture.
The ewes are eager for the summer range
and there is an itch as well in trail hands
to be on their way.
They hitch the sheep wagon to the pickup
saddle the horses, and head out.
The lambs must be pushed to cross Cherry Creek.
They are newly docked and can find
no sense in so much moving.
Now the difficult ascent up Cherry Creek Hill
so steep its ruts throw trucks
like a bronc bucks cow hands.
The old one recalls from his boyhood
a supply wagon headed for the ranch.
Old Tony Eli couldn't hold the team.
The wagon tipped, scattering their provisions
and the life of Tony Eli
down across the cinnamon colored mud.
Every year they meet his memory here
coming down too fast as they go slowly up.
They camp the first night atop the hill
inside a cloud and wait for the fog to lift.

They are up by four and on the move again
while the air is still cool and the sun
has not yet joined their climb.
By now they are all held
within a chamber of sound—
the choral bleating of moving sheep—
ewes and lambs in constant vocal contact.

Soon sound pulls the wagon
and orders the dogs
and sound becomes a canopy
which rain must penetrate
before it can hit their slickers.
Within the Conestoga of sound
they head toward Rock Creek
where barn swallows nest in the cliff.
Here there was always a drift
sheltered by an overhang.
Maggie would make ice cream
for her little ones, vanilla and some sugar
mixed with the last clean snow of winter
enjoyed under warm sun of late June
by a creek so small the children
could catch brook trout with their hands.

Once they reach the main stock trail they hear,
within the bleating, the rumor of a tinkling
harpsichord from the ghost saloon.
As if lashed to the mast they must face
forward past the phantoms of fancy ladies
in red and black dresses and scented tresses
who waited at "Chancreville"
for their busy season.
They were other-worldly apparitions then
for the smelly herders who held up there
on top of the world, weeks away
from other people, and easily forgot
they had sheep or cattle to keep track of.
Many an angry trail boss found his herd
all mixed up with unlikely company
while his herder or cow hands did the same.

At a lamb's pace they trail forward
into their manhood, into their prime, into their aging.
Passing all indecision and unknowing
they trail into the power of each person
who, trailing clouds of glory,
once came down and knew where
he was going in the shaft of morning light.

They trail into their memories, their
separate and mutual mountain childhoods
their storms, their shelters, their hunts
their stares into the eyes of wild things
the places where arrow heads emerged
from the ground before them like prairie dogs.
They trail beyond their individual worries of the day to day
from remote worlds that do not border this one.
And always they are swept along
on the air of music, the aggregate bleat
of a thousand eager-to-nurse lambs,
a thousand mother-assuring assonant calls
repeated, ceaseless, to the end of the trail and beyond.

They trail from the confines
of their own biographies into their blood lines.
With ancestral memory encoded in their genes
they take on the struggles of Mormon settlers.
Their legs bow and shape to the saddle.
Their eyes become snow blind.
Their arms and backs ache from salvaging
the smelly wet wool off carcasses of ewes
ice-chained to the grass in a sudden summer storm.
They have trailed back through their century
into pioneer battles with the elements.

They know the almost-mythical homesteaders
who left only the gray decaying timbered
remains of their one-man cabins
and a single name to tease these trail hands
into half-intimacy with long-absent lives
and troubled, tethered souls.
So when they bed the sheep at Fisher's corner
they sense the gun-toting presence
of this hermit whose once-clear mind
had taken in too many seasons
of solitary beauty that had no outlet
but grew like a tumor in his head
and shoved all social sanity aside.
And there's some old Billy
whose surname is forgotten
but whose preference will not be, for he
chose to homestead the huge open meadow
full of buffalo wallows where, early in the fall,
eagles teach their young maneuvers
from the rocky outcroppings high above,
wings wide and motionless on thin air
over lush green feed on Billy's Flats.

They pass the abandoned gold mine
where hopes of prospectors sparkle in the ore,
talk of miners echoes from scant remains
of stamp mill, and gold colored lichen grows
on the silent scattered stones.
The loyal ghost of Ed Madison's dog sits
on a rotted sluice box
with a fire wood log between its teeth.
They trail out of their race
into the origins of their occupation,
to the early days of domestication.

They are nomadic and Biblically beautiful.
The mouth harp shapes itself into a flute
and the ancient war with predators
becomes their own.
They are watchful for fox dens.
They listen for coyote howls
stand guard for the black bear
who stands upright as they
and is hungry for their sheep.
Their mindfulness is the sheep's only shield
from the mountain lion and the timber wolf.
They must arrive with the same sheep
they began to trail. No run-backs.
No losses to snow or coyotes.

At night they sleep with the lamb
born in the sleet storm, found in the fog,
revived by the fire, fed on a bottle
till they can find its mother in the morning
by the bloody bag she drags.

They trail through sage and timber,
through meadows of lupine and hillsides
of yellow daisies
over quartz and flint and moss agate.
The hooves of sheep stir up burnt umber dirt
that is tilled by prairie dogs
and fertilized by elk and deer.
They go back across the campsites
of Dull Knife, so brave it was said
his leathery skin would dull a dagger.
It couldn't dull the honed revenge
of the Seventh Cavalry nor the roar
of the fire that set ablaze

the sustenance of his people,
the winter's buffalo robes and meat
sent up like signals to haze
the clear November sky
from the funeral pyre of Cheyenne glory.
A necklace of fingers rattles in the pines
like wind chimes, and, after a gully washer,
small mysterious white heart beads
lie on the surface—red around the outside
and white in the center
like the bloodless white hearts
behind white men's promises.

They trail over homestead land
and Indian encampments
into the ancient medicine wheel
of the people before the people
whose chants and rituals are petrified into stone
as the sap of the huge timber is rock
and fish of the waveless ocean are hard and brittle.
Having moved inside the sound warp
backward across time,
they have trailed beyond culture,
over slate and fossil-bearing rock
into primordial newness of the earth.

They come in altered
to the gulch the ewes know well
where sheep will mother-up and bed down,
where five generations have herded their sheep
when snow has melted and the grass is high
and run-off has exposed more arrow heads
around the cabin at the end of the trail.

Mouthing-Out

Summer over on the mountain,
grass turned brown.
Before the herd is trailed back down to winter range
the men mouth-out.

Strategically placed to maneuver the chute,
a man grabs each temperamental ewe as she runs through.
Only the old guys,
the ones with eyes honed to sheep teeth
can look and instantly decide,
pull back her black lips and know by the incisors.

This is how they cull the herd,
choose which old ewes will get sold–
those that can't hack the trail back
to the badlands.

It's a ewe's teeth that make her
compliant with the ranch,
that say if she can stay
and the land sustain her.
With front teeth too worn
or starting to break, too brittle to take another winter
on the woody brush of salt sage, she'll have to go.
Even ground down, old teeth
will serve for a few more years
on the easy feed of Midwest pasture land.

Do you suppose a sheep rancher keeps looking back
over his left shoulder on the off chance
there might be a Commissioner of Sheep
to drop by for surprise inspection
peer into a guy's mouth and give the edict
that he no longer has the teeth for it?

Litany for a Rancher

for Frank Tolman, Dec.28.1998

Bless this man who lies abed
with so much riding on the way he dies,
Bless his riding the range, his bronc riding,
his riding it out, letting it ride,
riding herd on, riding rough-shod over,
and sometimes riding the fence.
Bless his fence building, fence fixing,
his offense, defense,
nonsense and his sensitivity.
Bless his camp tending, crop tending,
pretending, his tenderness
tending sick lambs at night,
his tending to park at the Ten Sleep bar,
his being wrong and his being right.
Bless his bull breeding,
bull-shitting, bull-dogging,
his shooting the bull
and his humble going home.
Bless his fishing, hunting,
dogging the timber, sheep dog training,
curses blaring, pups birthing,
nursing into dog days of his
doggedly caring for sheep.
Bless his lambing, docking, shearing,
his mouthing out, his dressing out,
and his being out of time.
Bless all that husbanding and the wife
a lifetime at his side.

Bless their siring of a dynasty.
Bless their dancing at the Wagon Wheel,
his sheep wagon,
covered wagon leading the train,
his being on the wagon and
the wagging tails of his well–trained dogs.
Bless his logging and cabin building,
the cab of his pickup truck,
his wethers, ewes, his bucks,
his cussing and his cussedness,
his luck and his being down on it.
After tending his land and tending
to land on his feet,
bless his recent forgetting, falling, recalling,
calling out in the night,
his victories, feats, defeats.
Bless his branding cattle, branding sheep,
rounding and rounding up,
rough riding, rodeo riding, riding high,
riding west into the sunset. Bless him.

Brush Fire

Ranchers burn off sagebrush
when it gets too thick
and threatens to choke range feed.
This was more smudging than the land would ever need—
redundant cleansing of rarified air
in a girlhood already blessed in being there.
We were children still too innocent of place
to imagine ourselves outside an encasement of safety.

On one still mountain day of recollection
excitement was stirred into our play
by the collective work of men,
work we heartily tried being part of,
delighting as we were in summer-yellow flames,
the way gruff, boisterous herders
teased and controlled them
like a litter of playful pups—
        till they grew
    and a wind came up
  and the timber approached.

Faces of the men went grave.
We were pushed back
in a flurry of desperate activity
as hot and full of noisy passion
as the ravenous flames,
            intent on their own purpose.

As I see this family
self-destruct before my eyes,
I think of that day
and other times I've noticed
how events, once set in motion,
can break constraints of the wills
that engendered them,
   can take on an identity,
      usurp authority,
         and burn
  headlong
     toward
   their own conclusion—
to ends, be they purified
     or base,
smoked over by the all-consuming fire.

Leaving Both Children and Land

Which is, for a patriarch, the worse curse,
a blood line that evaporates, dwindling
to a last stream trickle that seeps
beneath smooth stones in an arroyo
till his vast legacy
remains with none of his name to claim it,
or offspring that flourish
in the geometric progression of generations,
seeding the countryside with progeny
who will deepen in attachment to acreage
as they widen the gullies
and canyons between themselves until,
in the end, ancestral holdings,
parceled out in scrabble squares,
disperse like cottonwood fluff
and the spread is divided
while childhood memories of progeny,
like restless souls, hover over places
where they no longer feel welcome?

One Hundred Year Old Herd

It was a hundred year old herd.
Best in the country.
Trailed up from Utah
by Mormon forefathers
this band of sheep, first to cross
the cattlemen's "deadline" in Wyoming,
began to shape the land
that would feed them.

Making their bedground
on homesteaded flats,
these sheep were part of the proving up
part of the forming of family
the yarn that loomed them together
and fringed their edges.

Sheepmen each fall would match ewes
to their landscape,
choosing those most suited to the ranch
that was suiting itself to them—
large, open faced Lincoln breed,
hearty, disinclined to be wool-blind
or snow-blind in a spring storm,
tough as mutton with their full matted fleece.

For a finer wool,
buy a few Rambouillét bucks,
breed more delicate fibers into their hides.
But stay alert as a border collie
watching the lamb crop.

Keep only the open-faced ewes
with clear, peripheral vision
of their rust colored cliffs,
bentonite badlands,
lupine meadows of onion gulch.
Don't perpetuate wool hanging
in their eyes, clouding their picture
of where they are and why.

Slowly, down the century,
in increments of seasonal tasks—
lambing, docking, trailing,
mouthing out, breeding again—
these men, like masters of old,
sculpted a self-refining band of sheep
that grew through the generations.
They made their herd a thing
as proud as their name,
as fine as their families.

Some big Colorado outfit
that now owns them
will never know their herd's biography.

This summer the mountain range,
like an open sore, waits in vain
for the balm of their bleating.

Desert on the Tongue

This sibling rancor
draws the moisture from a conversation
the way choke cherries dry and shrivel your tongue.
Each year the child in you tries again
to see if they taste as bitter as dimmed memory suggests.

Our grandma knew the formula
for choke-cherry jelly—
boil down the bitter purple juice,
add lots and lots of sugar.

I wonder if she can sweeten this
from where she now observes and cringes
long dead in this ground and dry
as a mouth full of wild choke-cherries.

Ranch Family on Family Ranch

On ancestral land with these people
despite differences among us
there is a basis of place
that stands under words.
It is a ground of being
on which we have walked
and have sure footing.

Rim rocks frame our seeing of sky.
Behind the dusty road that goes away
and always back again,
rust clay cliffs rise iron fast
as past trustworthy standing,
wall in our spatial memory
and the delight eyes take
in gray-green sage and grass.

In such company
we know where we stand.
These are the people with whom
we are close
because of how closely
we know the same land.

WILDLIFE AND LIVESTOCK

Cabin Packrat

He takes into safe keeping
a pop-top ring, a shard of broken glass,
a pale topaz oval of fragrant sap,
an opalescent beetle's wing—
whatever catches an afternoon's shaft of sunlight
on the ground amid browning pine needles.

Sometimes a missing ring turns up
late spring, in a cabin cupboard
with an array of shiney finds
preserved from the world's carelessness
in a tuft of mattress stuffing.

Lacking his attention to light,
we laugh at the worthless bundle,
but the packrat gets cozy
in the back of some new neglected drawer
and, scurrying out about the timber,
notices what gleams.

Caring for the Crow

His shriveled lower limbs hang there,
in the way of his torso. We apply comfort,
but comfort is not night's freedom.
He partakes of majestic raven essence

but not enough, and he knows this
in the very air-marrow of his hollow bones.
Too soon expelled from heights,
too much of earth between them

and the possibility of flight, his great wings,
like strong arms of a double amputee,
are reduced in their duty to scooting
him on the ground. Strong of voice

and hearty of digestion, he has no choice
but to use his few responsive muscles to throw
back his head and open crimson stalactite
cavern where his double-terminated tongue,

emerging like the spear of a hunter,
draws game down into the gullet. This inertia
of living mocks the gentle hand of death.
He will eat and eat and only

his perpetuating potential will thrive.
Death has already claimed his flight.
We who have cared for him are invested
in our own ability to make him whole,

but it will not happen and I tell my husband
who knows, too. "The vet could inject it,"
he says, but I will have none of it.
Are we so long off the ranch? "Recall,"

I tell him, "What it was like to live daily
in the service of living things—with what
grace death would follow you into the barn
to do what you had to do." We were raised

out west where death rests with tools in the shed.
On the ranch we would not hire someone else
to slaughter our chickens or shoot the coyote
who has scattered a hillside with dead lambs.

Urban death has grown irrational as hail stones,
rides astride stray bullets, familiar with malicious whimsy.
Afraid to engage her as night nurse or scullery maid,
we forget with what kindness she embraces those in pain, undone,

how she redesigns misaligned bodies to corn or morning glory.
Here we do anything to keep from meeting her eyes.
But I am the one who says this so I am the one to do it.
This nursed crow deserves from me his first and final flight.

I take him out back and sit on a stump stroking the black
of his deep, obsidian darkness. He knows what the two
of us will do here and does not ask for food
but stares at me with his long, straight beak

slightly open as if he would say something, the filmy blue scrim
of his side-closing lids sliding across his eyes like a trap door
to a place of holy knowing. Having forgotten how hard
this can be, I lose philosophical certainty.

I have a piece of bailing twine for his fine, strong neck,
but I am weak with weeping and death can be proud,
reluctant to come at our bidding, even to visit her henchman.
When he is finally limp in my hands, his bottom

lids pulled up like the blankets of a child
tucked in for the night, I lay him on the stump
to find a shovel and dig a proper hole
in the sandy soil of our garden.

Dolly's Family Tree

The first cloned mammal was a ewe named Dolly
and from her were cloned Polly and Molly.

Dolly was not called into life on a midwinter hillside
by the muttony lust of a buck, rutting his future
into the sheepish receptivity of a ewe's usefulness
under the watchful eye of fragrant pines.
She was summoned by science,
insinuated down a cold glass tube
that would precede the uterus of unmother ewe.
This mother-father-sister-daughter, now mate
to herself was lifted whole from cycles of regeneration.
How many steps removed is she
from the god of natural procreation?
Her sibling-daughters, Polly and Molly,
our new Pharm animals,
model farmaceutical factories of the future.
Their milk will administer its extra protein
(human factor 9) to clot the independent blood
of hemophiliacs. While their cells'
will-to-division was attended with solicitude,
they were unlambed from before their birth.
How much will their DNA recall
of the way lambs leap with abandon across sage when
early May sun creeps over the rim of red clay buttes?
Do they all carry in their matching bones
a secret insoluble sadness at this lonely fact:
their making was no sheeply act,
but the lustful coupling of science and commerce?

Stalking Woman and Bull Elk's Eyes

She kneed a slow advance across grass and cactus,
palms tingling, belly brushed by sage,
seeking, that mountain evening,
proximity to the herd of elk, feigning a lack
of shape or manner that would send them running
back into the timber.
She fantasized acceptance, and the drive
like blind peer pressure, compelled her to assimilate,
to share their feeding ground at dusk, and earn,
in one illusive instant, their half-trust.

So she snaked up a draw
cracking brush, swishing over Bromegrass,
sloshing into marshy soil by an unexpected spring.
Crossing vacant spots with grass still matted
where they'd lain, she paused for seconds in their beds,
imagined they might join her there, recline beside her
to affirm a shared belonging.

As she moved into the clearing
where preceding dusks had drawn them,
the herd had silently descended from thick timber
to this lower meadow where she'd hoped to meet.
Sensing a presence, she raised her eyes to see him there
already sizing up her strange, spread-eagle form, her lusting gaze.

He took her, motionless and silent, in his power,
cradled her as infant in his rack that spread like a tree of life,
and held her captive in his eyes,
gored and left her whole, ravaged and restored her,
devoured her and gave her life again,
swept her through darkness in his own dilated pupils,
to light and back, through ages and the ties that bound them,
back through other epochs
before his sacrifice to her dexterity,
as her eyes locked into his,
became his eyes and saw her seeing him.

She never freed her watch from his
and yet she saw it all, the angel-hair clouds
that glowed reflections of the setting sun,
the evening star ascending from behind the pines
that framed him in a darkening outline,
lightning flashes that mystically renewed his power
to keep her there, willing prisoner of his grand hypnotic stare.
She barely knew who she was and where,
but darkness was around them as she rose and moved again,
her eyes still held in his pupils that had merged with night.
By the time she stood on the very spot where he had,
he was gone,
or out of sight.

Raccoon Visits

Our mutt must have some coon hound blood
that wakes him up when the old mother coon
comes foraging for his food on the back porch.
He rises up from a sound sleep,
yelping like a stuck pig,
and runs to the back door
to warn us of her intrusion.
Unlike those cubs we trapped
and resettled in the forest,
the fat furry bulk of her lumbers undisturbed
by his howling on this side of the door.
Incognito behind her black mask,
she rummages through our stuff,
and saunters towards the neighbor's
only when she's had her fill
of the dog's supper.

Having Tread, as Birds, the Air

He knew he was due for some kind of change,
having spent bent time working just to maintain
the way a mountain bluebird treads air,
flaps light-sky-inspired wings
in a gust and goes nowhere,
flutters above the brush in a stationary pocket of space
until something shifts—
purpose, wind, the flow of divine attention—
and it suddenly flies off, melding tone and intent
with the pale blue sky.

Encounter

Walking down along the creek, we hadn't noticed Zach
not lumbering at our heels when there came a peal
of high pitched shrieks as from a frightened child.
A terror-struck streak of brown, too large for a rabbit,
too slim for a calf, ears back, skimmed the ground
followed close by Zach, a clod of furred delight,
sporting in his warning bark. His tired old heart
recalled the chase and pumped pursuit into arthritic limbs.

We lunged for the dog, our threats mingling with shrill pleas of the
fleeing thing. As my friend dragged Zach back
to the cabin, I crept up cautiously upon the thing defiled.
Down in the grass where it must have collapsed
was a fawn. Eyes wide and glazed-over
with its final fright, it lay beside lavender lupine,
and nothing moved but my hand slowly
reaching to touch the soft young wonder of it.
I stroked it timidly so as not to startle away
any life that might have lingered in its fragile form.
Then I edged under it and sat,
pieta, with dangling limbs hanging off the too-small
cradle of my lap, my tears absorbed into soft, white
bulls'-eyes along the steep ridge of its spine.
A mere few drops of atavistic coyote blood
in our docile dog had offered over this proximity.
I could do nothing but suspend in an awe outside of time.

The doe paced in the timber at a safe distance
as if in a hall beyond intensive care. How dare I
stand and walk toward her with the lovely, lifeless
warmth of her child in my arms? How could I answer
for our intrusion into the playground of their meadow?

As I held it, it began to quicken against me
as each child against the other wall of my womb.
The bell clapper of its hanging tongue pulled back
into the head that still tolled with its fear.
Lids closed and opened again on large dark sighted eyes.
Breath came in and out of the leathery black nose.

Suddenly, where I had no right to be, I was
holding a thing I dared not hold—a live fawn.
My very smell was a threat. I rose and set it over
the fence where the watchful mother had leapt,
then walked toward the cabin thinking of how
the doe would come and begin, with her paint brush tongue,
to whitewash over our awfulness.
She would lick life into it as she had done after its birth,
lick my curiosity from its bushy white
undertail, the toxic scent of my body's oil
from its hide, lick my adoration from its dappled coat,
my whispered remorse from its huge, refined ears,
lick from the air around it the hot, predatory breath
of our dog. It would stand on its fine, delicate legs
and shake off death as Zach shakes lake water
into dry summer air.

At dawn I walked back to see, where I had left it,
(Ah, life's undaunted fervor for itself)
nothing
but an empty patch
of matted grass.

Border Collie

Her ears twitch and cock,
static in a short-wave receiver,
receptors of commands the herder barks
in his talking-to-the-dog voice.
Go way 'round and she does,
out and around the bunch of ewes,
roping them in with the unseen lasso of her trajectory,
her path on the periphery of their path.
Anticipating the erratic intentions of sheep
the way sod-busters read storm clouds,
she works the herd forward and,
while they are on track,
drops to the ground
fast as a prairie dog disappears into its hole.
From down in the sage, inert as a boulder,
she crouches slowly forward
making sure she does not scatter
their cohesive movement,
haunches with caution out to the side
of the swatch of slope the herder intends them to take.

But when one cussed ewe breaks away
and commands come with curses,
she is released like an arrow,
ears back, her black and white hair
streaking behind her sleek speed
till she has returned to the herd
the ewe and those that followed it
and reports her alert obedience to the herder's side.

Lethal White

> *The paint colt that is all white will*
> *also have an incomplete intestinal tract.*

Lethal white they call it, the gene
that imparts this fatal beauty,
an Overo paint with no spot, no hint of visible flaw,
white as Dakota in the moon of the lazy sun.
Legendary purity, born as if it would portend
the Great One's justice like the white buffalo,
letting the tribe envision a new generation
of brave striding it bareback into definitive battles
with another imperfect whiteness.
A vision-quest image of a spirit-stallion on a cochineal cliff
empowering a people with his majestic stance.

Some white is itself ambiguous—
white on green of a late spring blizzard,
white noise
white lies
white-hot wanting.
Some white calls you to trust
and cannot be relied on.

Hopeful as the owners
about his beating the odds against survival,
the paint mare licks him clean
warms him with the music of mother-breath
nudges him upright with her nose.

A pinto could live with balance,
tension of darkness, shadow,
patch of brown,
some color to ground it to reality.

Born as it is
pure mythical white
it cannot complete digestion.
By nightfall
they bury it on the bluff above the river
near the tribal dead.

MUTTON TOUGH & WOOLSACK SOFT

Two Step

Hartford, '43. The big band clubs swing
with doomed youths sucking nightlife
into their wartime daze.

He is another soldier on furlough who
cuts in, out, as always, for a good time.
She is a key punch operator at the Aetna.

She wears high platforms that pump
music into the curve of her calves.
She will confess to me, positioning

Dr. Scholl's squashed donut pads
over her corns, that her youthful vanity,
via those shoes, ruined her dancing feet.

He is a handsome cowboy who can dance.
What chance does she have?
He has two-stepped her out of the canteen

and onto her porch cot. She is not,
nor will she ever be, the only thing
on his mind, as he is hers.

The couch, white wicker with the weave
frayed, sends reed shoots in odd directions
like vine tendrils feeling for something rooted

to grab onto. The chenille spread
draped across the back covers them
from the night's chill as my mother,

with dark wavy hair and large coquettish eyes
that contradict her prudish piety, trades
the ruby of her wholeness for a pirate's chest

of longing buried in wet sand of her aspirations.
She has invited the future in, and it is hard
and unresponsive as this cot,

and yet, expectant as she soon will be.
They have not yet learned that charm
does not discriminate among recipients.

They do not know where the clarity
of her flashing eyes will go when
disappointment drops a dark scrim before them.

They are four years and half a continent
away from my birth. She carries my potency
in a pouch at her side like a gold doubloon.

My sister will join them soon. I am
waiting until they are surrounded by wood—
log cabin walls with pine forest outside.

I cannot be enticed into city matter
even by his charm
or the dark, flirty flash of her Irish eyes.

Gee, It's Great

Our living room—
Queen Anne furniture,
cornices over floor-length drapes,
rock-work fireplace. She had
planned every decorating detail
with post-war excitement about
what was to come, with the energy
of a generation that had subdued Evil
and should now be capable of anything.
She had brought Hartford into the badlands,
and her kitchen floor was an immaculate
maroon testament to her distinction.
Never mind the pickup parked outside
with a ewe and two lambs in the back,
nor the boots of insensitive in-laws
tracking mountain mud and sheep manure
over her sculptured wool carpeting.

We'd been sitting on the Duncan Phyfe divan
reading "Lazy Jack," about how the buffoon
applied experience and his mother's
good advice to all the wrong situations.
        She started singing,
"Gee it's great after bein' out late,
Walkin' my baby back home,"
then added a line without breaking tempo or tune,
"I used to play that on the piano,
Walkin' my baby back home."
My sister and I, four and six,
got tickled, looked at each other giggling,
then began to belly laugh.

She let herself go, and we all three
cavorted around in laughter
as in down released from
ripped ticking of a feather bed
and settling white and airy
over our innocence.

We were young and still hopeful
about the mother-daughter experiment,
had not yet begun to chip away
at each other's womanhood,
nor clog the free flow of possibility
with debris of our disappointments.
My mother was prim and proud and straight-backed.
She was beautiful and had not yet forgotten it.
She was set apart in her head and in her house
from the ranch around them.
She didn't know how far
she really was from Hartford,
farther still from Ireland,
and the brogue laughter
of her own sweet mother.

It was probably the most fun
I remember our having together—
this young bride in her perfectly decorated new house,
with the seeded lawn in the middle of a horse pasture
beginning to take root outside the draped windows,
and her two little girls
laughing with her uncontrollably
over liberties
she had taken with a song.

Kinesiology

My mother's unborn fetus
        rocking under
    the seashore moon
        of grandmother's
                    large heart
carried the very egg
        that would
    crack   open
and
        spill
                me
                    in.
No wonder I keep
    picking   her hurts off me
like   cockle   burrs,
that a body-worker,
reading my muscles
        like the
cosmic record of transgressions,
        asking
the strength of my arm
what it weakens
            under,
hears
    like keening
    from
    cracked windows
of a waking house
    the pivotal pain
of eight generations
    of Irish women.

Offering

There it rested
bold, straightforward,
the black-eyed-Susan
picked in the mountain garden outside the chapel
and placed by a bereft grandchild
on the dead woman's Adam's apple.

The child could not have known
it was her favorite flower
nor how her spirit rejoiced to find bearings
in the stark simplicity of it—
the dark-cored sunburst
grown in the ground she loved.
Its musty fragrance
must have pleased her hovering soul
more than the dozens of hot-house roses
breathing less of the archetypal flower
into the vigilant air.

Nor could the child have known
the comic relief it gave the grieving,
placed like a brooch of nature,
startling in vibrancy
as if it might spray water
into the face of the next mourner
to look over the edge of her coffin.
It jested its reminder
of the flower she began
to blossom into.

Loss

She stops chopping broccoli
and sits down at the yellow Formica table
sobbing guttural cleansing wails
that issue from a deep, unnamable pain.
She is home in her mother's kitchen
which she knows better than her own.
Her hand reaches to turn on the radio
that was always on the counter.
Frantically she searches the house
and finds it on the floor by her father's bed.
As a god restoring order to a chaotic universe,
she righteously returns it
to the kitchen counter and plugs it in.
It's a wine–colored Motorola, surely as old as she,
with two large black dials
that give it the look of a geometric gremlin
with far too much knowledge of the nature of things.
It should give out The Sons of the Pioneers
singing *Tumbling Tumbleweed*,
but it doesn't, so she cries
because she can't find her
mother's cabbage grater either,
and because Randy Hillhouse has died
and she didn't even know it,
and because her mother,
who would have told her in time,
is also dead, and because
the god damned Podunk radio station
probably doesn't even play
Tumbling Tumbleweed
anymore.

Sleeping in Mother's Studio

A dry Wyoming sunrise winds like switchbacks
around shades drawn to keep it out
as I awaken in her studio
full of yellow light and the paintings
stacked against walls, hung in rows
piled on the closet floor,
paintings that whispered to me
all through the night of the silver dollar moon,
weaving their shapes and hues into my dreams.
Their pigment intensities say more than any journal.
My mother never had a valid voice,
except, perhaps, the resonance of green and blue.

This morning flowers demand I notice them,
an impressionistic vase of red poppies
against a muddled background
of undistinguished shapes
frames filled with peonies
too full of weighty loveliness
to hold themselves erect
a globe-shaped bowl of yellow roses
on a white lace table cloth.

There are restful still-lifes
so quiet you could walk inside
take an orange from the table, retreat again
and not disturb a thing. A white porcelain
teapot is ready to serve whomever ventures in.
And there, beside a bowl of fruit, is the same
glossy purple eggplant I ran into like an old friend
in Renoir's "Fruits from the Midi" at the Art Institute.

Looking down at me, beckoning me into her dark eyes,
is a dignified young girl in wide-brimmed hat,
a limp rose in her right hand.
She has walked through fire
and her delicate, pale green frock
is endangered by the red that blazes around her.

Now they all speak at once,
each one asking my attention.
See what I am, the light on dark,
dark on light, distinguished brush strokes,
delicate, controlled, precise;
screaming brush strokes, brash and angry,
disapproving of what they have formed,
table tops that don't connect to a ground,
flowers suspended without stems.

Know me, they begin to shout.
See me as you never saw.
Come closer; you are near-sighted.
Let your eyes redeem
the deaf ear you always turned to me.

The self portrait of a white haired young woman
with a widow's peak and deep dark eyes that cannot lie
hums softly of light on dark,
dark on light, cadmium against cerulean.

Now I hear them. Barefoot women
with baskets of fruit on their heads
chant the banter of the market place.
The stucco Colonial Church sets its bell tower ringing
while a crimson Madonna cries
over her scarlet baby
and the canvas beneath her eyes is damp.

Father Places

He was stretched to rarity
with intentions in dark ancestral earth
and desire that eyed the flight of migratory birds,
a heart at home with family
and feet that followed dancing girls
in those exotic places even he could not pronounce.

I learned about the world
from the war-time photos of a gentle man,
about our backyard, a mountain,
as its mysteries unfolded
through explorations at his hand-held side.
We watched a stink bug roll its egg-filled
ball of dung along the dirt.
I was a child taught timber biology
by a man who'd seen the Taj Mahal
mapped the expanse of Africa
been greeted at his palace by Haile Selassie
mugged in dark streets of Marrakech
and remembered dancing girls
in more strange places
than I could put names to.

Betrothal

There are men,
and one such is my father,
whose first love is the landscape,
who pledge to it their heart
with such ardent devotion
that they will never descend
to need the human beings who walk upon it.
Kindness, justice, toil, even romance
they can offer,
but not life-love.
For they remain ever faithful
to the bond of soul
they sealed early on with the land.

At Home in the Wild

for Dean Tolman

He was born with and into a kinship with critters.
As a boy he carried into the sheep camp
frogs, snakes, prairie dogs, and an endless
succession of magpies and fledgling hawks.

He has stared straight into the face
of the mountain lion
that carried his eyes' identifying
back with it into the wild.
He has known the most majestic of animals
that walked the earth beside him
or in his sights.
He has trapped and tagged and hunted and bagged.
He has shot and dressed-out and grown strong
on the flesh of the fleet and antlered.

Yet he has also nursed, tamed, doctored, saved
and freed the most needy of injured beasts.
He knows their homes and habits,
what they feed on and what they need,
what spooks them, what calls them to you.

He has felt between his thighs
the desire of an Arabian stallion,
sire of half the foals in the countryside.
He has broken horses and his own bones,
ridden broncs and the range,
pulled from troubled wombs
calves and lambs encased in amniotic safety
that would soon have smothered their emergence.

He picks up vermin by the tail—
skunks, porcupine, rock chucks, snakes—
grows remorseful from their anger,
and sets them on their way again.
He has tracked the mountain goat of Alaska
and buddied up to an ill-tempered badger
in his own backyard.

He has taken into his feet
the sure-footedness of mountain sheep,
in his lungs their need for lighter air.
His home is the lion's lair,
the bear's den, the elk's high meadow,
the antelope's expanse of badlands.

How do I account for the heartiness of this hunter,
that he grows more tenacious
with every life he takes?
that his hold on the land
he shares with these animals
deepens each time he pulls
a warm coiled snake of entrails
out onto browning grass or pine needles?

This benign blood-lust of the hunter
is something that we cannot know,
those of us ill at ease with killing,
those of us unwilling, as well
to risk our own health and comfort
bringing it to fellow living things.
Has this facility of killing and bolstering life
given him an insider's place
at the table with Death,
death that knows who can't be taken by surprise?

Perhaps a century of bull elk,
seeing deep into the windows of this man's soul,
transferred the land's mandate that he be upon it.

His killing has made him one
with so many things
that he is spread across mountain meadows
of the West.

When he dies,
before he sees white light,
will he look again into the eyes
of wild things whose living and dying
kept him upright?

Once he's gone into the ground,
deer and elk will graze his grave,
prairie dogs will mound and tunnel among his bones
and be at home in him.

Parkinson's

for Dean Tolman

The oldest of seven, born steady despite
dreams dormant behind his eyes, he was an
iron-fast anchor that kept the family from drifting.

Now his fingers worry the air as if messages written there
might be grabbed before they float away on particles of dust.
The hand hanging flaps and flails like a brookie in a creel.

His petal foot wafts like a loose wheel about to spin off
and go rolling downhill. If illness is metaphor,
what is the meaning behind my father's shimmy

as if some limb or appendage wanted to dance
while the rest of him decided to sit this one out?
A jumping bean soul squashed in the pocket of a stable life.

That old restlessness that would have had him on the move
was compressed into a solid marble column,
a pillar shoring up what rested on or against him.

Did forty years of a shaky marriage give him this tremulous
bodily way of being, as if old indecision in his cells
has him quivering long after the fact of that rash proposal?

That time of steadfast standing required such force of will
that wavering worked itself into sinew of his unbent frame.
While he stood at attention, an independent foot

learned to tap of its own accord. This agitation
will wash him clean as a creek-scrubbed garment
hung to bleach in the sun, though he may quake the earth
when it opens to take him back.

Season

Lately he shares with me
the waning of his strength.
On days when the pain is worse
he contemplates staying in bed—
not seriously,
just plays with that strange, adolescent
notion of a day well spent.
But he always wills his bent frame upright
and gets on with what he would do.

It's October, one last hunting season.
This year, he says, the gun feels heavy.
He won't be toting it up slopes.
He'll lean across the hood of a pickup
and hope his keen eye and steady aim
will suffice.
But he's getting ready,
that's the thing.
He's getting ready.

Night Fishing

Reel of the well-equipped angler
hooks me, tugs me out of a sound sleep.
The Bass Show is blaring in the next room.
I doze, incorporate scenes of casting
into my dreams.
Down pillows of my childhood lure me back
to the clear lake of oblivion
till *a dandy on the line*, fighting,
yanks me awake.
I toss and flop in the bed—
troll shallow waters where his memories flow,
Soon I'm casting in mountain streams,
reeling in that rainbow.

My father should be put to bed.
All the lights in the house are on.
The late night outdoor channel shouts.
I expect to find him fantasy fishing
exotic salt-water spots of the world.
But he is slumped in his chair,
drifting in the soundest sleep
he will have all night
and catching his limit
in its deep waters.

Meeting at Home

We have come together around a man
more bent than we remember
slower than has been his customary pace.
Here we drink from the mountain spring
of his having stayed,
having sanctified a place
by so long and so wholly being in it.
Now his slowly growing needs
are the family home
to which we return again and again
to be fed.

In the Path of the Forest Fire

My grandmother held
in the starry night of her memory
this land in all its hungry newness.

Now there's a pine tree as tall as I am
growing right through the bed springs
that litter the ground like severed weed vines.
Some debris is still black from the forest fire,
while all the metal rubble
has rusted to the red of old blood.
Bromegrass and lupine have replaced
the wood floors of her cabin.

Here she taught and nurtured, mended worsteds,
fit her work to their play
when hands that tugged at her hem
could not lure her from tasks of the day.

Overturned and glittering in the green like fool's gold
is some chrome trim from the wood stove
where she cooked for her family of eight.
Once, when the creek flooded,
and she gathered her brood uphill,
she sent daddy to crawl in the window
and fetch her bread from that oven before it burned.

Her work of transformation, like the earth's, was hard.
Goaded by a father-in-law
who knew nothing of her insides,
she got up to cook for shearing hands
one red morning
when an expectation faltered.

She pinned rags across her pelvic floor
like a diaper to hold back the hemorrhage.

Flattened beneath a charred old pine
that's nearly become earth again
is the kerosene lantern
by which she read her <u>Book of Mormon</u>
when the others were asleep.

Saplings and shooting star
have obliterated lines of the walls,
and proud walls they were,
the hand-hewn logs a tribute to the men
who felled them in the timber and fitted them
like colored layers of this land's geology
piled up into a home.
Within those walls she crocheted and knitted,
tatted her longing for the dainty and delicate,
pieced her softness and her warmth
into a coverlet of the foregone
to throw over her loved ones
on cold mountain nights.

Would she have been disheartened or relieved
to see this green outlive her floor,
to know that where she scrubbed her knuckles raw
would now provide good feed
for the sheep her offspring tend,
sheep that, like hearth fires,
have been their love and their labor,
their knitting and undoing,
their nemesis and their security,
the focus of their wild and woolly lives?

A Dream of Living Coal

for Maggie Hopkin Tolman

It was black, they told her,
shriveled, necrotic,
dead inside her for weeks
and poisoning her system like nightshade.
She'd have died within days, the doctor said,
had she stayed on the mountain with the sheep.
She owed her life to the team and rig
that rumbled her delirium down the
rutted trails to town.

For years she would dream
of grabbing from the fire
a glowing cinder
in the shape of a baby.

My Grandmother's Skin

Many is the baby
who has blessed her flesh
and redeemed her flabby
wrinkled skin by
having once
pulled it taught
across his coming
as lovers do
a comforter
in February storms.

Before She Left

for Maggie Hopkin Tolman

When I was a girl Grandma
didn't go to the mountains anymore.
I couldn't understand it, and I'd call her every time,
We're going to the mountains, Grandma. Wanna come?
She was gracious in declining, and her voice sloped away
like the rutted road toward the creek.
Naw, Honey, you go on.
Bring me down some lupine, though.
I asked Daddy and all the herders if they knew why.
It seemed to me a place so pieced of the fabric of her soul.
Her blue flowered apron
hung on a nail by the cabin back door
and the plank by the water in the spring house
was smooth from her knees.
Her quilts covered every mouse-eaten mattress
that muffled squeaky springs
and her red checkered oilcloth was still on the table.
Her whistled gospel tunes
blew in the window with the smell of pines.
In the granary, where she stayed
that first spring before there was a cabin,
the door still hung on leather hinges
she had made in desperation
by cutting up a harness one doorless dusk
to separate her children
from the hungry timber noises that come out with stars.

Something of her was everywhere on the homestead.
She birthed on its table and corseted herself
behind the cabbage rose curtain
hung on a rod over the doorway to a tiny bedroom,

year after year, in a world of men.
The cabin's comfort was her plumpness.
Its bread was of her kneading.
Hers was the taming of its wildness,
the endurance of its harshness, the proving up on its acreage.

She gave it her youth and its next generations
and was somehow content not to go back.
Her modest house in town had running water,
sweet peas snaking up the siding
and thin tea cups in a china cupboard
so unlike the dipper hung over the rim
of the galvanized metal bucket.
Did her curly willow fingers
recall decades of diapers washed in icy creek water?
Did her memory leap like a sheep dog at the sound of an old pickup
that went to town and didn't hear the train?
Had her weakened pelvic floor, too many times,
endured bouncing up the washed out roads,
first on horseback, next in wagons,
then in the rattley army truck
brought back after the war when her boys came home?

Maybe she had no need to return,
carrying it around in those mountainous breasts, no longer corseted.
I know, at least, before she left
she crocheted onto meadows of lupine
the ecru sinews of her youthful strength,
taught forget-me-nots to whisper their names
from the tiny yellow centers of pastel blue and pink,
tatted the ridges of pines with her joy,
and planted for us on hillsides of wildflowers,
seeds of her fullness.

PEOPLE OF SAGEBRUSH COUNTRY

Recollections of Place

Long before history books,
before memory took form
in the changing shape of human consciousness,
recall was housed outside the body
in monuments and temples and almost liquid motion
across walls of caves.
Places were the storehouse of events
and called them back into the present in the presence
of one who was there to recollect.
Triumphs and terrors of a people
stampeded like phantom buffalo
into the mind of she who stood staring
strangely stirred by events she had not lived.

In Wyoming it's still that way.
A map reads like a parchment chronicle
of wild and unresolved events.
When you stand on the landmarked scape
uncertain feelings hover over you
like a motionless hawk, about to dive.
Strange stories strain to tell themselves in you.

By Crazy Woman Creek you speak in incoherent rushes
of her confusion and their cruelty.
In the vague vicinity of Lost Cabin
the lust for gold begins in empty jeans pockets
and sinks down in your soul
the way specks of color settle to the bottom
of washed black silt in a miner's pan.
Along the banks of Dead Horse Creek
its long bare bones have sprouted cottonwoods
that fling, high into the air each spring, the woolly ghosts

of dust that trailed its palomino hooves.

Some towns you pass pass on to you
what some had hoped to gain in settling there;
Reliance, Recluse, Superior, Lost Spring.

In Sundance the flesh that guards your heart
is pierced, your courage is strung to the pole,
blood colored dust brushed up by circling feet
clouds the air, and screech owl chanting
fills your ears from inner out.
On red clay cliffs the massive hooves
of buffalo thunder under you, while your limbs
weary with the work of preparation
and your belly fills with the feast that will follow.
Near Hanging Woman Creek you begin knowing
things you'd rather not and the itch
around your scar conveys how one man's justice
is another's crowning infamy.

And sometimes, when mountains turn impassable backs,
and hail clouds gray and blacken heaven,
the fears of frontier families
pass over you like cloud shadows across badlands.
You feel how the aging earth
stores more than bones and the sandstone shapes
of life in the ancient withdrawn sea.
She is the stone green monument
to the life and death her slate records.
She is your memory and,
like an old woman's,
often sharper in the long ago.

Pioneer Spirit

Perhaps it was not the land,
available for the slaving for,
nor the absence of
        established order
that made them bold,
    daring, capable
        of hold-on bravery,
inventiveness, endurance.
    I'm not sure it was
    anything less than
        this uninterrupted
        eloquence
        of sky.

High-Necked Lace and Rightness

They're tearing down the old farm house
across the black top from the Hawkinson 80.
I walk up the lane and see it standing
squarely on its strong foundation,
still white and proud in the afternoon sun.
They've torn apart
the barn and sheds for weathered wood
but nothing of the human dwelling
is designated worthy to be saved.
I bear no kinship with these men and women
who lived here and, for whatever reason, left,
except perhaps a feeling for the beauty of the place.

The house seems only partly still and empty.
From the upstairs rooms I almost hear
the residue of a house full of racing children
and the working men, smelling of onion gulch,
their threshing machine voices scraping
across piano music—music fit like well-coped corners
into sparse empty moments of the once living women,
with their high-necked lace and rightness.

We always imagine them to have been
other than we are, those mysterious, solemn women
in starched and ruffled cotton who baked the bread
and birthed the babies and held our great grandfathers
through their follies, stalwart in their silent affirmations.
Their stern fragility solidifies, silvered on daguerreotypes
that render their lives a rightness we're still striving for.
Could any have been petty or in some sphere incapable?

The floor slants a little where the piano stood.
The pine that frames the doorways
and windows facing out onto the fields
is clean as on the day when it was hewn
except for notches noting growth of children
who long ago attained their father's stature.
Forgotten on a closet floor amid mouse droppings,
preserved in a vault of dusty cardboard,
are the woven hand-worked garments of another time.
Like curious raccoons in new sweet corn
I'm drawn to this box that holds
textile remnants of their femininity—blouses
so demure no skin could be detected from beneath,
no trace of touchability show through;
rolls of crocheted lace
cut from worn-out garments to be used again
a pair of sleeves of pale green apple silk
with delicate French lace
a baby's bonnet, woolen long-johns
full gathered white lawn petticoats
a stained apron with its ruffles
white and starched—the kitchen garb
of women in the stories old men tell
who canned and survived winters worse than ours,
who worked the fields beside the men and drove the rig
but looked as delicate as china
in the pictures where they do not smile
but rest a helping hand upon the shoulder
of some equally serious man.

I touch the past with the reverence
of a child alone in the sanctuary after Mass.
Under batistes and linens lies an archetypal dress
of soft pink flowered voile,

the clothing of an apparition
with rows of sego lily lace and, at the bodice,
illusion so fragile as to disintegrate
at the crudeness of my careful touch.
The dress must surely have had sewn into its seams
the threads of every virtue we might seek.

I put it on.
My fingers fasten tiny buttons
as I take a breath to shrink my waist to size.
Strangely, in this pinkness I'm no longer
separate from the ladies in the pictures.
I feel both their uncertainty and strength
and now I know.
Their legs ached often and their lower backs.
They went off by themselves and cried
quietly into goose down pillows.
They made errors in judgment.
In anger they said things to children
that in darkness they'd regret.
They wondered, doubted, feared; they longed.
Their rightness comes from all these things.

Churning Butter

This was the meditation of pioneer women,
this hour of mandatory inactivity,
a leaving off of scrubbing grubby faces
grass-stained muslin, wood plank floors.

They savored the quiet time to sit, churn, and ponder
how moving something turns it into something new
as they watched the frothing up of thick, cloud cream,
folded into it the energy that flexed their milking
muscle just below the elbow. They wondered
at the invisible process of becoming by which
a thing long-traveled, even if only in a circle,
changes imperceptibly.

The cream being turned at shadow's lengthening
along the trunk of the cottonwood outside the window
is already other than the cream which was skimmed
off the bucket at dawn and poured with stored jars
of yesterday's cream into the gallon glass churn.

A little freckled girl with disheveled curls comes calling,
Momma, go. Myron's stuck in the hay loft—
scared to climb down. I'll churn while you fetch him.

The children know a process, once begun, cannot be left.
So if one child needs a mother, another has to spell her,
take over turning the handle that turns the gears
that turn the paddles that push the cream.
What if I stop? the girl wonders, but doesn't dare.

It amounts to compliance by rote, her follow-through.
And once having assumed the duty,
she is bound to continue that same rhythmic cranking,

bound by the need of the task itself,
the fact of being the one there to do it.

Dang it, that mean gander is after Amanda again.
Dean, get over here and take this churn.
Like the ferryman forced to row back and forth
until he can put the oar in the hands of another,
the child, who now must rescue a sister,
cannot slack off until she has conscripted a sibling.

As thick waves slosh against shoulders of the jar
he daydreams, this little one drafted
into connectedness with butterfat, wonders what
would happen if he shifted to the not-so-tired-arm,
reversed the jar and began to turn the other way.
Would he churn it right back to sweet cream
and have to start over?

Mother returns to resume duties just in time.
By now the shadows of branches spread farther
on the deep-grooved bark of the cottonwood
and fat has begun to collect on the rod.
She is glad to be back at it.
It calms her, this ritual of dairy transmutation.
She anticipates that instant of metamorphosis
when cloud white cream becomes sun yellow butter
floating in a sea of buttermilk.
She has always been in awe of cream
how well it holds its mystery, encoded record of revolutions.
Like the boy, she wonders
if its only time in motion that matters
or would a changing of directions
unfold what has become enfolded?
She's never tried it. She hasn't time.

Seamstress

for Hazel Shelton

Hazel was a seamstress with a feel for fabric
and the way things fit, with a flare for mischief
and what to wear for the next adventure.
She taught me sewing for 4-H and Make-it-with-Wool.
In those years when I thought ineptitude
had been invented to accommodate my mother,
I could escape to Hazel's sewing porch
where colored threads scriggled like hieroglyphs
on the carpet and arms of chairs
and you didn't dare walk barefoot for the pins.

She had come north with a reliable Singer machine
that she'd never replace and the light,
always ablaze above her work table,
was an open invitation to the gaiety of a flapper's delta.
What did I know of southern belles?
Had she lived like Zelda, or Tennessee Williams women?
Though I'm foggy on details, stories sped with fast cars,
rash decisions, breathy laughter trailing behind
like Isadora's scarves.

As I cross-stitched hems and sewed bound buttonholes,
Louisiana of the thirties jazzed itself into the room
with all its risk and chanciness, single minded horns
blowing vast holes in sweltering gardenia-scented nights,
gowns cut on the bias and clinging across protruding hip bones,
see-through chiffon and satin that absorbed the light,
and the oil man who danced her through it all,
then swept her away out West.

Sam was an imposing figure of a man, tall as an oil derrick,
now white haired and still good looking
but sad as a zoo animal,
his territory reduced to the four-block radius
between his recliner and the bars. He'd greet me
with the charm of a southern gentleman
then retreat beyond the range of the feminine.

But Hazel and I had good times
around tailoring tutorials, facing interfacing.
I learned to hide the knot and bury the loose ends,
to adapt the pattern to fit exactly,
means of adjusting—gussets, pleats and darts,
ways of making things hold to your dreams,
like basting, bias binding and reinforced seams.
My waist was thin as a fairy princess
when she fitted me for the prom in a bodice
so tight as to assure I'd be breathless all night.
She knew secrets about design,
fitting into and realigning. She could have
dressed me to be at ease on Jay Gatsby's verandah.
Events like that didn't happen in Wyoming
but she had me blossom like magnolias
in our high school gym and become the princess bride
in a charmless brick church built in the fifties to get us by.
There wasn't much Hazel couldn't do
except, though she withered trying,
mend the seams of a man who retired young
with nothing to do with his hands.

Fossil Hunting on Sheep Mountain

Sheep Mountain,
its geology tilted up toward vibrant sky,
exposes indiscretions of its making
like an ill-bred family.

Air is savory with salt-sage.

The devil has shed toenails
all over this hillside.
Fossils gravel gray ground
telling how the softest things can harden,
how the fluid stones itself
to permanence of form.

An arrogant white twister,
so far away its fierceness appears design in animation,
drills its fury into innocent counterpoints of pine.

Tiny worm-like pieces of coral
mosaic the surface of anthills
alongside small agatized bellemnites
and minuscule crinoid five-point stars
as if the archetype of warheads
could not avoid the design of flags and children's drawings
eons before life emerged from the sea
and now both stars and bullets
are returned to us in stone.

Paleontology

Sandstone layers beneath dry air
store eons of the world's growing up
like a scrapbook of pictures and pressed boutonnieres,
each page another stage of the developing child,
another milestone in the coming of age.

Here the primordial sea has scattered
agatized recollections of fluidity—
turritella clusters of sea shells, cephalopods,
baculites like puzzles of once-life
fitting together in stiff sections—
all hardened onto badlands as if,
like Lot's wife, the living waters
looked back once too often.

Another layer and jungle ferns
and the teeming green abundance
of hot, moist vegetation lies flattened into shale
as in a lovesick maiden's flower press.

And then, as earth's memory quakes
at the impact of their giant footfalls,
the leviathans
quick in their coming
quick in their ferocious devouring
quick in their dying away.

The Paleozoic wants to reveal itself to her.
She has an eagle-eye for finding
like St. Anthony, patron of misplacers
incessantly searching for something lost.
But these stone bones of the prehistoric past

are not really lost, just hiding into rock
for millions of earth-altering years.
The pages of their pressing call for many layers
but they are here, washing to the surface
like a scant remembered dream that wants
our time for its recall.
Come, they say, *Dig. Dig carefully;*
brush the dust from me with a fine instrument
and I will teach you something.

From a ravine one knob of femur shows its
gray-black surface, beckons her into Jurassic past.
She begins to chip away ages of bentonite badlands,
chip away the sandstone layers that imbed it,
chip away shale and mica schist,
millions of years of the earth's gradual moving on.
She feels like Michaelangelo
removing from marble everything that is not the David.
This graceful shape of bone,
once honeycombed and cored with warm marrow,
held up some giant life that knew this place as its own.
Now its hardened memory of form
excites her blood to race.
It is deep in the ravine
and will take days to dig.
It is bigger than she could lift
were she five times her size.
It is older than she can think of
and more strange
but it has exposed itself to her
and she keeps on digging.

Geology

A poet works like geology
heaving, in great cataclysms,
the inside out to the crust
thrusting mountains out of the ground
icing great bowls into
the known surface of the world
layering air until something
tangible has stratified itself
saving leaves, ferns, dragonfly wings
into stony wholeness
geoding captive liquid
into pointed facets of amethyst light.

Executive Order

February 19, 1942. FDR signed an order
which allowed military authorities to exclude
anyone from anywhere without hearings.
This set the stage for the evacuation of
Japanese Americans from their homes on
the pacific coast to 10 inland relocation centers.

With internment in the Zeitgeist,
we readily took up the archetype of concentration,
a barbed wire forged of fear and righteousness.
But don't we all rest easier when what is different
is securely tucked away?
We could herd people into barns
where they might have viewed the livestock
when they brought their vegetables
to last year's county fair.
Each horse stall or chicken coop
could house a family.
What need had they for privacy?
Were they not passing perilous secrets
like a virus among themselves anyway?
And the hot manure odor from hay
beneath makeshift floor boards
could mingle in their lungs with latent sabotage
that pumped its mal intents into their limbs.
All these yellow people,
under suspicion for the size of their eyes,
too close to the water, too close to their "homeland"
(only two thirds native born Americans)
were safely put away and watched
from guard towers with omniscient views
and we all slept better for it, did we not?

Heart Mountain Internment Camp

population 10,767
third largest city in Wyoming in 1943

The butte forms a crude, irregular heart.
Indians knew it as a landmark.
For days across dry sagebrush
they could see it waiting, its curved
upper lip on the horizon welcoming
them to the bubbling, hot
medicine waters of Yellowstone.

Internees could not see the heart
nor the promiscuous lips of peaks
kissing the independent sky.
From where they gazed,
vesica eyes glazed with disbelief,
it resembled Devil's Tower.
It teased with expansiveness
like the lights of San Francisco
from the dark proximity of Alcatraz
and cast an ambiguous afternoon shadow
across four hundred sixty-five tar-paper barracks
spread like a bedground of buffalo
over the grassless flat. No,
the heart of the mountain was not
discernible from their vantage,
only its fortress sides rising from the plateau
like the guard towers surveying their relocated lives.

But living in close confines was customary.
They could make a town of a prison,
pioneer a place, bunched tight against
more open space than their island forebears
could have willed into existence.

They could bow and begin again to build—
school to teach all these children should know,
hospital to heal, though deepest wounds go invisible,
newspaper to tell what the world enacted outside,
graceful homes within each small, bare room,
six families per colorless building,
a tea ceremony pot packed away
in a leather valise under a cot—
all anger and loss like *onigiri* rolled tight
as the thinly diced sushi inside a clean
white buffer of rice.

Ikebana of sage and cactus blossom,
embroidered red silk wedding kimono
sometimes taken out and touched,
were the only colors in their lives
other than the wide blue sky
that bent above them to transfer
a kiss of consolation from the heart lips
of the remorseful mountain.

Issei Mother at Heart Mountain

This child will never see his mother's birth soil.
And now he is taken from his own.
She must find a way to plant his round toes
in this ground like potato eyes.
This dry earth is fertile, wants only water.
She will irrigate and vegetables will grow.
This delicate-boned woman,
scalded like a silk worm
from yet another home
goes about the work of transformation
with a willful embrace of duty.
Because she is who she is, where she is,
she obeys the state as she might
a demanding, suspicious, ill-tempered
mother-in-law,
obeys her with a strangely heartfelt love.

Heart Mountain War Memorial

May the injustices of the removal and
incarceration of 120,000 people of
Japanese ancestry during World War II
never be repeated.—memorial plaque

Issei enlisted, were eager to go
from the barbed wire prison
with its two guard towers
where sentinels of distrust,
the armed eyes of a nation,
watched their movements,
guarded their lives
but turned away from their deaths.

Nisei and Sansei fought
against their forefathers' homeland,
defended their country,
the state that didn't know them,
that was threatened by their presence
but would accept their sacrifice.

A weathered wood monument
lists twenty-one internees who died in the war
but names are no longer legible.
With scant Wyoming rain from the wide blue sky
their names have washed into thirsty soil.
With winds blowing off the mountains of Yellowstone
their names have flown over farms of the Big Horn Basin.
We have breathed their names in the dewy air of sunrise
and eaten their names
in our Jap stand vegetables.

Seventy-Fifth Annual Hyattville Old Timers' Picnic

Cattle have been herded uphill and the pasture mowed
to ready the spot for neighbors from three counties.
A side of beef roasts on an open fire and coffee bubbles
in blackened copper boilers while old timers talk
about the fishing and the feed, the market and the lamb crop.

Children have rolled their Levis and are walking stones
in the creek or climbing the massive cottonwoods
with bark like topographical maps of mountains
that lean over the water. The low slung junipers
and shag bark cedars that shelter cattle from July sun

now shade the blankets of the picnic guests—
these fiercely loyal friends whose play is as large scale
as their work, as spread out and unfettered as their stock.
Huge rough planks nailed to weathered timbers form seats
that wait in this meadow for these once-yearly occupants.

Today again they seat old timers and the ranch hands
and their children and the friends now listening
to the fiddler doing *Foggy Mountain Breakdown*
over the creek's rolled *rrr*s of rushing mountain run-off.
Mr. Rea, oldest pioneer still here, is given a quilt

made by a woman eighty-three. His daughter explains this to him
where he sits in his wheel chair surrounded by offspring.
A smile of recognition wrinkles his brown cheeks.
This is his ranch, his empire, and he is ninety-six years
weathered by the work of it. Now sluggish of hearing,

he is cutting-horse quick of mind. A red haired toddler
follows a teasing hopper that escapes her into the weeds
so she fingers the rust-colored dirt she has caught
and which blends with her hair as she scatters it into the breeze.
To the north, red cliffs guard thousands-of-years-old secrets.

Petroglyphs etched in canyon walls tell similar stories—
the social life of ancients camped by healing waters,
mysterious peoples long gone who taught by other initiation rites
respect for the elders, gratitude for the land,
hope for the lives of the young who carry on.

A Hundred Years Later

This is rodeo time in Thermopolis, Wyoming,
its main street tumbleweeded with dancers
booting their bent-kneed bodies through
Texas two-step and western swing.
Toddlers edge between couples like cutting ponies.
Little girls twirl together, their new boots
smooth against cooling pavement.
Feedlot hay bales surround the crowd,
offer the tired a place to plunk down.
Neon at the corner just says BAR.
That's enough. Cowboys
wander in with an empty, out with a full.
Like the bull, this music keeps them moving.
It's country with an occasional Elvis.
The band, set up on a flat bed in front of the bar,
is Indian. Every enigmatic high-cheeked face
a native of this basin; Arapaho, Shoshone, Crow.
In T-shirts and baseball caps
with stage drums and electric guitars
they play requested tunes
sing the melancholy lyrics while sacred waters
of their fathers flow into the swimming pool
      and cowboys and Indians dance.

FACES IN THE LANDSCAPE

Pack Trip

It can't have been the way your horse
    was flirting
with the pack mare as we slowly wound
    trail circles
round the mountain till they
    cork screwed
to the center of our lives,
    not that
has kept me near you all these years,
    nor even
the outline of your strong young frame
    against
high sky at sunrise.
    It may be
all I guess at of your secrets
    after
I've revealed the worst of mine.
    Perhaps
the evening star reflected in your eyes
    inviting me
to swim deceiving depths
    despite
    all warnings.

Initials Carved

I walked
the creek alone from the lodge
to the bridge before the last switchback,
ignoring, this time, the blood-red stems of dogwood
and the sap-scented overhang of sanctuary pines,
questioning instead each quaking aspen old enough
to have known us then, before there were
the other lives to complicate the issue of our loving.
I sought from each that testimonial
to our passion and our youth.

But they were mute,
denying any knowledge of our secret visit there,
claiming never to have seen our tan and slender bodies
drinking sunshine by the creek.
Determined, I examined every one for wounds
that spelled our promises, our hopes and naiveté,
for scars like formed clay monuments
to a day when we were other than we are,
when we eagerly marred the clean-eyed whiteness
of its bark with letters of our linkage
and the simple addition sign
meaning we might multiply.

I hoped
to see the geometric evidence
of our violence to it long ago,
protruding, as I knew it would, with age.
Its keloid malformation would remind me
of that fragrant fresh-scored bark

and our first mountainous ascent,
when we left our mark on the tree
after leaving our mark on each other.

Then one stood out at last
as if it could remember
being tattooed like a sailor
drunk with the spelling of his lover's name.
It proudly displayed the hieroglyph,
gray and bulging with age, to show how,
down the years, it gave up an even surface
to perpetuate what it had seen in us
on the day we defiled it.

                    I closed
my eyes to read with finger tips
the Braille record of smooth flesh
damp with spray from run-off creek,
wild raspberries still fresh in shared mouths,
sunlight threading its way to your cheek
through balsam and shimmering aspen leaves.
Having found it, I felt suddenly relieved.
If these weathered letters spell you love me,
I won't argue with a tree.

In the Landscape

It's late afternoon and the boys have saddled up
to bring sheep in from the high meadow.
Tomorrow they'll begin trailing them to the mountains
where extra rain has made the grass stare upward,
unusually alert as if put on guard
by bountiful attentions of a sometimes tenuous lover.

For the moment nothing needs them
so he takes her by the hand and together
they go out back to climb the accessible part of the cliff,
the color of their daughter's hair in sunlight.
The red wall is discreet with its secrets
of outlaw comings and goings, of Arapaho bands
and their landmarks, of fox dens littered with dead lambs.

When there is no more footing,
just a solid, impassable cliff jutting up into blue sky
like a flaming wall of the underworld
broken through the crust of earth, they turn
and sit there where domain spreads out before them—
a diorama of snake gray gravel road
side-winding through green pastured hills
and sagebrush buttes to snow-hooded mountains.
Down by the creek omniscient cottonwoods watch
over a dwarfed ranch house and log bunk house
with half its old sod roof eroded off.

They sit silent as archangels surveying
the workings of a world in their charge
but active with wills of its own.
Far below it moves in slow motion
like a boy's toy farm come magically alive.

Border collies race around the red barn
and horses graze in fenced pasture.
The bell of the lead sheep, corralled
with the bleating bum lambs, clangs upward
to them, and sounds seem larger by far
than the animals that release them.

The yard is animated by small children
with armloads of sightless pups, all mouths
searching giggling necks and faces for a nipple.

Sheep come rolling off the buttes
like a low cloud gathering
with dogs altering its shape
as easily as wind in fog.
When a boy comes riding ahead for help at the corrals,
a line of little children ants its way up the lane
and places itself across the road.
The herd glides to where the fence of children
turns its lead, then quicksilvers through the gate
and forms out again inside the corral.

Observing from above, the couple is silent and full
as old gods undisturbed by prayer.
They are too far away to alter anything in the panorama.
It seems a scene self-contained once set in motion
like the enigmatic course of children's lives.
Chances are no one will look toward
the towering red cliff to see them watching,
archangels in the landscape.

To a Man of Few Words

Have you, then, chosen
to be a geode,
hiding diamond-shaped
and glowing under grayness,
desirable and prickly
with many shiny facets,
smooth, pointedly mute,
protected by simplicity
and dumb as crystal lead?

Apology to My Son for the Fact of His Birthplace

What may I expect for you,
my one-month-every-summer cowboy
whose rubber-toed red tennis shoes
will stumble up this mountain
not often enough to transform them
to the cloven hooves of Big Horn sheep?
And freckled nose,
scraped beyond rear end's bounce
from saddle to prairie dog mound,
shall have healed too long since
before riding lessons are applied next time.
But what of lamb-soft summer mornings
in the rainbowed meadow's warmth,
or dusty sagebrush days of chasing
strays into the herd,
the half dead wild things you'll love
to health and tear-sent freedom,
and turns of rolling down sawmill hill
to icy snow-melt creek that stops you cold—
all this remembered as a special time,
a different time, not home and all and always as to me,
not food and air for growing right and rural,
growing lone and night hawk free and timber tall.
This work for muscling-up manly thighs in gritty black soil
that I'd have had hardening your bones,
will be as fascination of a half-known foreign land
that lures out of its mystery
and not as home, as it has been to me.
Forgive me, if you can,
my one-month-every-summer (city) cowboy.

Maggots

Three companions,
mother and boys now taller than she,
share the same ancestral memories
flickering like fireflies
above the bed ground of conscious thought
as they cross the pasture and scale the fence
to nose around a homesteader's cabin,
one of many that protrude from mountain meadows
like pre-historic mounds, messengers from a former time,
slowly settling earthward like the girth of her grandfather.
Each cabin is unique, there having been no formulae
for how to fell the timber and hew the logs
or chink the cracks to hold out winds
that come moaning down the mountain
in the fall with the bugle of bull elk.

Rock chucks scold them for invading.
The boys must bend to enter
as each withdraws into a private fantasy.
Only she remembers the old ones who built them,
but barely, and to imagine how life was lived inside,
even she has only stories.

Content with what they've seen
and the sun's rose rays from behind the peak,
they begin the hike back to the comfort cabin
through lupine meadow and down toward the creek.

Assaulted unexpectedly by the smell of death,
they look for a body until it startles them
all at once with an eyeless stare,
the half-reclaimed carcass of a ewe

there by the creek where the clear constant rush
of moving water is the only perception
that does not offend the senses.

More full of motion than in life,
the ewe wiggles everywhere with maggots.
Ravenous and thorough,
they sing with the joy of their feast.
When a boy pokes a stick into a teeming belly,
they disappear by the thousands
and writhe forth in another part of the body.
It's an enticing, grotesque game
and the boys are new to the work of maggots,
the message and the mystery of maggots,
the strange hypnotic beauty of their hideous dance,
the way they make the skin on your shoulders tingle
yet you always watch.

In silence they prod and stare and shiver,
think a blessing for the ewe that will not
lamb next spring when the grass is
tallest and greenest in this very spot,
then start back through the timber to the cabin,
each with the crawling image inside
where it will wing and lay eggs of its own.

Gift

My firstborn son, child of high-rise forests,
urban urchin, spouter of street lingo,
is trailing sheep with my dad,
herding the seasoned ewes and newly-docked lambs
from the buttes to mountain summer range.
Home for the summer I've sent my boy,
the boy I was not, the boy my father needed
to ranch in his bootsteps
learn stones and animals
build fences and future
hunt with his rifle and ride at his side.
I stayed here in this overpopulated flatland
with my city guilt and sent my boy home
for my dad to be to him all I cannot,
to teach him the rituals enacted every year
through the work of herders, horses, sheep dogs, sheep,
to share his rodeo circuit tales
and ice water from a mountain creek,
the taste of venison cooked on a wood stove.
These men will ride together
through sagebrush and pine
and more than just my memories are there,
more than the injustices of their gender
and shortcomings of mine.
Something of the child I was not
waits at rock creek where they'll
camp and catch trout for dinner.

Something of the parent I wish to be
circles like a hawk over Billy's Flats
where they'll see that beads of the Indian grave
have sewn the ground with seeds of a culture
rich in respect for the land we came to after them.

Here in the city with my books
I must relax despite my lacking.
For all I could not be
to father and to son,
being daughter, mother,
I gave each one the other
he would not have known
without me.

DAPPLED VELVET HOURS

Cocoon of Winged Days

I stretch to live the mountain myths
engendered in the cocoon of my winged days.
I was unlikely goddess of the grass
that greened Olympian meadows
in the not docked newborn lamb
of my sheepishness.
I was cabined warm
spring house watermeloned cool
paint pod, chipmunk, snail shell amused
sibling to wild flowers
while running like the fawn into the forest
were my mummy worm
and dappled velvet hours.

Woman Becomes Heartwood

She'd always lusted after trees
as if she sensed the softness in her
needed to couple with the grain of oak,
or, as Druid priestess, knew who to worship.
As a girl she befriended the plum, plucked
and sucked bitter green wisdom from around the pits.
From where she sat on the shoulders of a lodge pole pine
that towered over the spring house
and lent her a view of the creek and the saw mill,
she first saw foresters and lumber jacks.
Hoping they would suffice, she tried loving them,
then carpenters, carvers, tree trimmers,
even salesmen in Christmas tree lots.
But men could not satisfy her longing.
Being held high in the arms of trees was never enough
and she was not content
living among their fragments in paneled rooms.
Many she loved from the ground up for their beauty
or their strangeness, their strength or their virility.
Then one dusk she saw it, a magnificent hollow oak
with a large hole at its first branching.
Secretly resolved to union that moon–washed midnight
she stripped on the grass, took the pins from her hair
and climbed to where she could lower herself into its very core.
Scraped by its rough interior, she bled into its side.
Touching its soil, her toes grew deep down
and she felt its sap surge upward in her as a kiss that lingers.
Raising her arms into the branches
like a bride putting on her gown,
she smiled into the darkness
as leaf buds formed on her fingers.

The Sound of Hollow

We were little girls with a ranch for a backyard
and fantasies scaled to its grandeur—
Indian princesses astride wild stallions,
hers white with black mane and tail,
mine black with white mane and tail.
And our hair grew one with the wind we flew through,
racing to cliff face to survey our people's invaded lands.

We were explorers in rough terrain
armed with pocket knives of fathers
and before an expedition
we agreed how each would suck the venom
from the rattlesnake bite of the other.

But some days we'd be out-bound orphans
who had found each other,
it was I dictating the tone of this world,
and we'd meet in the forest at a hollow tree.
What's that? she asked.
It's a sad tree. I guess at it.
In-breathing to our racing, leaping, climbing of trees
were these somber hours when we talked a lot
and hunkered low to the ground in fallen timber
practicing melancholy by instinct
choosing words for their sound
surrounding our bond with borrowed misfortune
and modifiers like *forlorn, abandoned, howling,*
words heard in fairy tales or the talk of elders,
hollow trees my favorite.
My heavy young heart could settle there
in the absence of concepts.

Meaning not perfectly acquired,
we drifted in the realm of implication, mood,
used to taking clues from a speaker's expression.
And here the gist was clear.
Lack and decline hovered
around the words like carrion birds.
Vacancy, void.
We met there,
in the hollow space of words,
the core of meaning gone
and strong, firm bark of ambiance
forming the resting place we nestled into.

Ghost Town

The scent of old cabins
holds me like a picket pin.
I do not want to walk outside
even into mountain sunshine.
It must be years of wood smoke
deep in the grain of logs
that fires forth my childhood
as incantations to the spirit of youth.

These were the very smells
that called me out of heights,
lured me into matter
the way a well-tied fly entices brook trout.
Sage brush and wood smoke were the incense
that led my seeking soul into a cabin conception
that I might touch to earth near timber line
as if not to come down too far.

I linger among sparse, functional old furnishings.
My tie to such places goes deeper than memory,
stored perhaps in some membrane around the heart.
There were always pictures in the water mark designs
on rough lumber ceilings,
pictures formed for me
by seeping in of summer storms.

These memories are fragile
as the burned wicks of kerosene lamps.
If touched, they crumble into
powdery ash.

In the Timber

In the timber
behind the cabin clearing was
a squirrel's cache that pillowed
up the ground with pine cone parts
between a once-tall fallen fir and the
tribute to its fertile usefulness, a huddled
cluster of aspiring lodge-pole pines. There
almost-infant I would fetal up among the
spongy, fungal still-decaying mound
with yarn doll clutched to cuddle
and sleep into the ground
in mindless intuition
of my sure place
in that space.

They're Coming

Now, after all morning's hope to help,
chasing lambs that worked through weak spots
in our wall-of-children fences,
fetching tools and water jugs
or trying to count fast to tally,
trying hard past trying to be useful,
shouted at like sheep dog pups
when our trying hard unglued the self-adhesive herd,
we felt it,
knew it half by practice,
half through instinct of our developing
sense of usefulness.

They're almost done, we hollered,
running, chasing dirt our toes had loosened
down the hill of arrow heads, eyes on
blurred ground going under, partly
to steady hurried feet from wind and gravity,
but more not to miss a flew-past relic
of a life more breeze free even than our own,
across the dusty rutted road
that had met Grandpa as a grassy
deer-to-water path and had, down the years,
inclined the wagon wheels and anxious
lambs-to-meadow hooves, truck tires,
and these, the feet of eager children
bearing messages.

We rounded the last curve to the cabin,
down through still-tall fall feed beyond that old corral
and that--which we tried so not to be--
long-years-useless, left-there wagon

that had been our play house, haven,
vehicle, and back drop to the detailed dramas
of busy child minds.

With practiced cautions we toe-stepped across
dodging-water rocks in the icy spring creek
that cooled us all the near-sun summer.
Dripping in and out of tangled bushes,
hide-and-seek willows rooting low to water,
we bounded up the path in one awkward
graceful bull ballet of pure intent,
through cabin door, and, panting,
proud, announced, *They're coming.*
The men are coming. They're almost done
mouthing out the last bunch now.
They're tired, hot and hungry.

Our mission fulfilled, we flopped down
in plank chairs to watch our mothers
drop flour–pounded venison into spitting lard,
dish up black skillets full of peppered onion spuds,
slice warm white oven bread.
Triumphantly we surveyed at last
the preparations we had set in motion
with the runner's torch—
They're coming.

Yellow Gold

We are happily lost. The tacit aim
of unmarked mountain roads is in effect:
if you don't know where you are,
you've got no business being here.
We women have a job—
taking supplies and grub to trail hands
for the pay-off of a summer day in the mountains.
But finding the moving herd is no easy trick.
At the ranch they have given us directions,
perfunctory ones, as if heritage must have
provided knowledge of all mountain roads
in the same recessive gene that produced
red hair and freckles, as if our very being here
has supplied us with a "compass for a brain"
like my navigator father had for aerial mapping.
Let's see. Fourth day out, they ought to be
about to Bear Trap meadows. Two buttes
past where the creek flows into that draw.
You know, the first road to your right
off the main stock trail.
We do not know, but no one has confessed it.
Vigilant in our calculations, we're not sure
what we're looking for, really—
a road that's an eroded truck tire rut
or just a place where this spring's grass
has been matted, tramped and driven over?
Pulled like a compass needle toward
what we will encounter, we take a chance,
turn off and struggle open the old fence gate
on what must once have been a road
but one that has known no hooves this season.

As we approach the crest of the hill,
an unseen meadow bursts, for our eyes,
into a yellow confetti chorus
as if a lifetime of old friends shouted in unison,
Surprise!
As far as we can see
is a gently swaying prairie of daisies,
balsamroot, snow thistle, little sunflowers,
all yellow as a brood of chicks
scurrying into a blur of moving sunlight.

This spread of butter has been churned by a wet spring
and might not coalesce like this again in our lifetime.
The sun hid here a stash of yellow
by which it might replenish in October.
It is as if the sacred trove of an Incan empire
had not been plundered, but sprinkled secretly
over this hillside to wait for our (being lost) discovery.
We women get out of the pickup
and sit down in the storehouse, chest deep
in deposited sunshine smelling of pollen freshness.
We are rich.
Silently we fill our vision to the brim,
stuff recollections with gold,
gather all the treasure our nostrils will hold
and climb back into the truck
to look for the turn off we must have missed.

Mountain Meadow in Bloom

All spring it had prepared itself,
primped, and practiced gold as if it were sport,
borrowed from the sun
and returned coins with interest,

tossed around yellow like a tennis ball.
Perhaps visible, unseen, perhaps not—
I shall never know—
it prepared itself and waited

for release into our viewing.
It was not whole until we
reached the crest of the hill
and gasped at the opulence

strewn over the ground before us.
We became gods,
surveying the beauty
we completed in the taking in.

It gave gold as if we asked alms
and was delivered from the waiting
by the praise that rose up through us
like the smoke of Abel's sacrifice.

Leaving the Mountains

In another useless try at sealing up the uncontainable,
I gather scents—juniper berries, pine sap,
balsam I can dry and leave out in a wooden bowl
to smell and be transported,
swept like a tumble weed
on a gust of homesick longing.

Pictures fail at squashing timber
onto 4 x 6 matte finish.
Nothing can substitute when mountains
have pulled themselves out from under me
and settled discontentedly into my yearnings.

What's missing is serenity of soul,
a sense of well-being centered where
blood and air exchange their vows and contents,
the harmony resounding in my mind's ear
with the rushing of a nearby creek,
that equanimity of will so needed
in the graceless overdoing of my everyday
when an hour's errand swells
like the days-dead carcass of a ewe
into an oversized and ugly afternoon.

It's then I'm in need of having held
in the very cells of my body
what this landscape is to me—
having internalized its arc like the
by-heart migratory flight of wild geese
or the skyward path to certain trees
encoded in a monarch's copper wings.

Firsts

If all the world
would glisten
like the sky
through mica
held before
a child's eye,
I'd have no reason
to lament the
dwindling
of days that,
for this fire,
had been the
kindling, nor
bemoan the distance
of the mountain
slopes which were
my first loves,
laughs, homes,
sins, suns,
hopes.

Nourishment

Reared
    on the taste
     of eagle eggs,
 I gummed milk teeth
    through
with pine sap
   and swallowed
healthy seasonings
  of black
and fertile earth.

Nurtured
   with bark
  and juniper berries,
I grew
    each day
less pale
  and never
    choked
 on fox tail
   till
I went away.

Come Home

I heard newly-docked lambs bleating
for their mothers as they bled
initiation into fence-free
leaps through life on open range
and I thought they called me home
again to mountains still unchanged.
And I thought they said,
The shepherd in your soul
must stand on range land soon.
Your feet will flatten walking concrete
till they can no longer grip a hillside.
Your lungs will choke exhaust
till clean, thin air can't reach
to nourish your extremities.
Your ears will close to sirens
till the gentle whine of breeze through pines
is henceforth only silence.
Your eyes will blink out soot,
squint into neon, and tear
until the clearest blues and greens
are grayed and undistinguished
where they wait.
Come home.

Backward Boots

When the riderless quarterhorse
was led into the arena,
the rodeo crowd went silent as timber wildlife
below forming storm clouds.
Hooves skied July dust
and air above the empty saddle
churned a barely-visible twister.

His boots were backwards in the stirrups
for his phantom to view what he had come from
like a child sitting with supplies in the buckboard
looking back over buttes they had rumbled up—
root-shaped cracks in the road bank
where spring rains had passed
taking solidity with them toward lowlands—
a boy watching colors flow out down mountain
from his vantage—cinnabar canyon, foothills,
sage badlands, and the grassy valley farthest off—
colors touched, by gradations, into vibrancy
by the spreading blue wand of dawn sky.

Going On

As the nursed fawn returns again and again
to the hand that held the lamb's bottle,
walks gracefully each time a little farther into the field,
craning its slender neck and training chestnut eyes
upon the gentle one who ministered to its former hunger
before bounding a last time beyond the meadow
and into deep timber,

so the dead turn their attention to the lives left behind,
in increments of months and years
less unsteady in their new terrain, slightly more
intent on finding their bearings on another plain,
by gradations more at ease
in the spindrift tide of archetypal thought
until they no longer need to populate our dreams.

After the Last Page

Life really begins on the morning
of the next white page
after the novel has ended,
after the motives of past generations
have twisted themselves like tubers
into the actions of the protagonist,
when violence has subsided in a denouement,
past the hurting and the working through,
beyond that flash of knowing in the last chapter,
the notice of something enduring
or strangely beautiful in the natural world,
when attention has been called
to the behavior of barnyard fowl
beneath a V of wild geese
or the stance of a wet stallion
on a ridge under an expanse of clearing sky.
When everything that mattered is over
and everything ahead is too mundane to tell about
but the burdened heart is still not finished
circulating crimson words,
this is where the story starts.

Acknowledgements

Grateful acknowledgement is made to the editors of publications and anthologies where the following poems first appeared or have been reprinted.

"After a Hard Winter," *Celebrating Gaia, Sweet Annie and Sweet Pea Review*: *Vermillion Literary Project* 1999; and *ProCreation*

"After the Last Page," *Treasured Poems of America*, Sparrowgrass Poetry Forum, Winter 2000 (first place award winner); and *Footsteps*

"Badlands," *Vermillion Literary Project 2003*

"Before She Left," *Eclectic Women, Sweet Annie and Sweet Pea Review*; and *Woven on the Wind*, ed. Linda Hasselstrom, Gaydell Collier, and Nancy Curtis, Houghton Mifflin, New York, 2001

"Big Horn Mountains," *Vermillion Literary Project 2002*

"Border Collie," *Prairie Winds, 2002*

"Caring for the Crow." *Evansville Review*

"Churning Butter," *Celebrating Gaia, Sweet Annie and Sweet Pea Review*

"Come Home," *Encore, Prize Poems NFSPS, 2003*

"Dappled Velvet Hours," *Hodge Podge Poetry*

"Dolly's Family Tree," *The Lucid Stone*

"A Dream of Living Coal," *Mid America Poetry Review*

"Encounter," *Barefoot Grass Journal*

"Executive Order," *People's Press 2000: Here's to Humanity*, Baltimore, MD, 99; and *Out of Line*

"Feed My Sheep," *Ancient Paths*

"A Force in Motion," *Petroglyph*

"Gee, It's Great," *Birmingham Poetry Review*

"Gift," *Essential Love*, Ginny Lowe Connors, ed., Grayson Books, West Hartford, CT, 2000

"Having Tread, as Birds, the Air," *Vermillion Literary Project 2003*

"Heart Mountain," *The New Observer*, Tokyo, Japan

"Heart Mountain War Memorial," *Hodge Podge Poetry*

"High Necked Lace and Rightness," *Higginsville Reader*; and *Vermillion Literary Project*

"In the Path of the Forest Fire," *The Eclectic Woman: Sweet Annie and Sweet Pea Review*

"Hundred Year Old Herd," *Illya's Honey*

"Issei Mother at Heart Mountain," *The New Observer*, Tokyo, Japan

"Jacketing a Lamb," *Heartlands Today*

"Litany for a Rancher," *Chachalaca; Vermillion Literary Project 2000*; and *Times of Sorrow, Times of Grace,* Backwater Press, Omaha, NE 2002; First Place WyoPoets, 2002

"Loss," *Carriage House Review*; *Vermillion Literary Project*

"Medicine Wheel," *Barefoot Grass Journal*

"Mentors," published as "Sheepherders," *Gin Binder Poetry Review;* and

Coffee & Chicory

"Mountain Meadow in Bloom," *ProCreation*

"Mountain Oysters," *The Green Hills Literary Lantern;* and *Fresh Ground*

"Night Fishing," *Owen Wister Review*; *Birmingham Poetry Review*; *TMP Irregular*, and *Vermillion Literary Project*

"Offering," *California Quarterly*

"Paleontology," *TMP Irregular*

"Parkinson's," *Square Lake*

"Ranch," *Illya's Honey*

"Recollections of Place," *Sweet Annie & Sweet Pea Review*

" Seamstress," *To Honor A Teacher*, ed. Jeff Spoden, Andrew McMeel, Kansas City, 1999

"Season," *Vermillion Literary Project 2002*

"Sheepman Dead," *Birmingham Poetry Review*

"Shot with Expectation," *Owen Wister Review*

"Sleeping in Mother's Studio," *13ᵗʰ Moon*, (Nominated for Pushcart Prize) *Eclectic Woman, Sweet Annie & Sweet Pea Review*

"The Sound of Hollow," *Pudding*; and *Remembered into Life*, Maureen Tolman Flannery, New Song Press, 1999

"Two-Step," *The Larcom Review*; and *Curious Rooms*

"Ways of Being Incorporated," *Gin Binder Poetry Review*

"Western Land," *TMP Irregular*, and *Vermillion Literary Project 1999*

"Woman Becomes Heartwood," *Poet's Edge*; and *Margins*

"Yellow Gold," *Times of Sorrow, Times of Grace*, Backwater Press, Omaha, NE 2002

Maureen Tolman Flannery
lives in Evanston, Illinois
where she and her actor husband Dan
have raised their four children.
Her other books are
Secret of the Rising up: Poems of Mexico
and *Remembered into Life.* She edited the anthology
Knowing Stones: Poems of Exotic Places.

Pen and ink drawings in this
book are by Cathy Mooses. She is a printmaker at
The Cooper Union for the Advancement of Science and Art.
With a group of young artists Cathy is founding an arts
collective and education center in Mexico
where artists and students will also serve
the community of Petatlan, Guerrero.